WHERE THERE

CW00872166

THE AUTOBIOGRAPHY OF
MIKE BRACE CBE DL: PART 1

Disability is a state of mind, my state, and your minds!

You can't change my state, but hopefully, I will say something that will change your mind?

To Mum

With thanks.

First edition published in 1980 by Souvenir Press
Second edition with thanks to David Levy

For further information visit www.mikebrace.co.uk

ISBN-13: 978-1723181030
ISBN-10: 172318103X

Copyright © 2018 Mike Brace
All rights reserved

Revisions edited by John Duffy
Printed by CreateSpace

Contents

ACKNOWLEDGEMENTS

I would like to acknowledge with many thanks the help given by the staff of the Stoke Mandeville Stadium in checking the section on the history and development of sport for the disabled; and also Mike Butler for allowing me to use his study on "Visually Handicapped Students".

My thanks must also go to the many friends, especially Chris, who typed the original manuscript for me, and of course to my wife Maureen for reading the proofs.

Chapter 1

Remember Remember

When I regained consciousness I was lying on the grass, with the smell of burnt flesh and gun powder in my nostrils and a warm sticky liquid trickling down my face. For a second or two I could not work out what had happened, but when I put my hand to my face and saw my palm covered in blood I remembered, and realised that I was badly cut.

I had been playing football on the local common in Hackney, near my home in East London, when I had seen a small group of boys huddled together looking at something on the ground. As the ball went out of play, I ran to where they were gathered and as I arrived, they dispersed. On the ground, and the evident object of their attention, was a black medicine bottle with the lid screwed on tight. I bent down and picked the bottle up and was reading the label when it exploded in my face. I had vaguely heard someone say "drop it", but had taken no notice until it was too late. The date was Wednesday, 2nd November 1960, and the cause of the explosion, a banger inside the bottle.

I rose to my feet and began to run home, with my friends racing along the road with me. I remember an old lady saying, "Have you cut yourself son?"

My reply was none too polite for a ten-year-old lad. It was something like "No, I always have blood, running down my face you silly old…"

As I entered my street I remember seeing my aunt on the doorstep talking to a neighbour. I rushed past her and into the kitchen, where I filled a basin with cold water and plunged my face into it. It was then, I think, that I realised just how serious my injuries were. The water turned immediately a very dark red and no matter how many times I emptied the basin and put my face back in, the water continued to turn red.

At that point a neighbour came into the kitchen to look at the cuts. His alarm was obvious, and he offered at once to take me to the hospital. At this point I could still see normally and thought that I had merely cut myself badly. I walked with the neighbour to the car and he drove me to the local hospital. My aunt said she would phone my mum and let her know where we were, and I remember being concerned that she be told not to worry, as I knew that a phone call saying I had been injured would frighten her half to death.

On our way to the hospital my vision began to blur slightly and I began to feel violently sick, but I managed to hold out until we entered the Casualty Department. I was shown in to the doctor at once, and began to feel more and more alarmed at the serious faces and obvious anxiety all around me. The doctor called for the nurse, and I was laid on a bed with cotton-wool pads placed over both eyes, which increased my anxiety. At that point the nausea grew worse and I was violently sick into a bowl. Within a few minutes my mother was by my side and I could tell from her voice that she was worried too.

Next I remember hearing the bells of an ambulance and a sister or nurse raising her voice at the ambulance driver for taking his time, saying something about someone's sight being at risk. But still I did not really link the panic with me. I was then lifted into an ambulance by the driver and my mum climbed in beside me. I was being taken to Moorfield's Eye Hospital, only a few minutes' ride away. I remember saying to my mother as the emergency bells rang and the ambulance sped along the road, "All we need now is Dr Dawson and we would have Emergency Ward 10" (a popular television soap at the time).

My mother did not manage to laugh much and I was sick again.

7

The next few hours are very vague in my memory. I remember being wheeled through the hospital and being sick several times. I had had minced meat for dinner and the awful taste of regurgitated mince will linger with me for ever. I must have passed out or have been sedated, as my next recollection is of waking up in the middle of the night. Everywhere was quiet and I found myself lying in a bed, cotton-wool pads over both eyes, bandages round my face and nobody, as far as I could tell, near me. At this point panic overwhelmed me and I called out. The soft voice of a nurse tried to comfort me, and explained to me that I was in hospital and that my eyes were bandaged because one had been cut by a piece of glass.

I woke several times during that night, feeling disorientated, frightened, tired and confused. In the morning, I was aroused or should I say woken by, two nurses who said they were going to give me a bed- bath. I must not move my head they said, and told me that I must lie as still as possible and then they proceeded to wash me "all over". This experience I found uncomfortable and embarrassing. I still had the taste of regurgitated mince in my mouth and vowed that I would never eat the stuff again. Little did I know then, that because my eye condition required me not to move my head, or chew things vigorously, all I would have for my dinner for the next few days was minced meat.

As I lay there alone, in the dark and still slightly sleepy, a voice from the next bed asked if I was all right. It was strange at first, having a conversation with someone you could not see even though he was only three feet away. Roger, I learned, was twelve and had a twin sister and a brother. He had been in for over a week and had had an operation for a squint. He chatted almost non-stop and soon we became friends. During my week in bed he would often read me books, or the letters which my school friends had sent, and describe what was going on in the world outside our window. Roger helped to relieve the boredom I would otherwise have suffered, and gave me no chance to lie there brooding over what had happened.

In the two or three days following the accident I saw a doctor several times. I remember very clearly the first time the pads were taken off. I was absolutely terrified and completely unable to open my eyes. When the doctor tried to shine a torch into them I screamed and fought him. I could not explain why I felt like I did, but I suppose, subconsciously, I was frightened of what I would (or would not) see. My self- imposed blindness lasted for three days, until my uncle bet me ten shillings that I couldn't open my eyes by visiting time the following day. Whether I was driven by a real need to know whether or not I could see, or by a love of money, I do not know, but the next evening, when my mother turned into the corridor leading to the ward, I saw her and waved to her. Her face, which up to that moment had appeared older than I had remembered it, suddenly broke into a smile almost as quickly as she broke into a run. I could not understand her extreme pleasure just because I was able to open my eyes; but I cannot remember her ever appearing happier. I stayed in hospital for over six weeks and my hospitalisation was an enjoyable one. I had perfect vision in my right eye and some vision in my left, though not enough to read with. I had been extremely lucky, everyone told me. I could read with my right eye easily and planned to go back to school after the Christmas holiday. The thought of school did not please me much, as I was to take my eleven-plus exam the following summer, which would decide my choice of secondary school and indeed affect my whole future. But at the time it meant only more homework and studying and less football and sport.

I left hospital on 14th December with considerable sadness. I had been kindly treated there, and I had indulged my high spirits in endless practical jokes on the nurses, which they took in good part. I also remember, just before I left, meeting a boy called Timothy. He was blind and had come into hospital for an operation to have a false eye put in. Timothy was an object of wonder and amazement. Even though he could not see, he managed to do all manner of things by using his other senses. He walked around the ward with no apparent difficulty, recognised people when they spoke to him even though he could not see them, and knew immediately what his food was by taste, even though at times it was unrecognisable to those of us who could see! Tim could also read books and papers with his fingers. He used something called braille, which appeared to me then only a mass of bumps and dots with no regular pattern or shape. The dots bore no resemblance to ordinary letters and had apparently to be written on a machine or with a "dotter" and a "frame", whatever they were. I was so fascinated with the braille that I asked Tim to give me a bit of paper with the dots on it as a souvenir. I thought Timothy was marvellous, and I was thankful that I did not have to read the dots like he did.

I was home just in time to attend all the Christmas parties at school and on leaving hospital, I could read the penultimate line on the eye chart with my right eye and the third line with my left. During the week immediately after discharge, however, I noticed that I could in fact see less than I thought. My eyes got tired easily, and when after five days I found it difficult to read any kind of print I put it down to this fatigue. But when I went back to hospital for my first check-up on 21st December, and was asked by the doctor to read the eye chart, I knew something was seriously wrong. With my right eye, I could just see the second row and with my left I could see only the large first letter. All the doctors' faces looked grave, as did my mother's, and I was left alone for a time while she discussed with the doctors my changed sight levels.

When my mother finally came over to me, she said that something was not quite right with my eyes and that the doctors wanted me to come back into hospital. I felt quite happy about going in again, but was less keen when my mum said it would have to be that afternoon. I did not want to be in hospital for Christmas! Why was it that urgent?

I was allowed, rather unwillingly on the doctors' part, to go home with my mum to collect my things and of course to change my underwear! To my mother, clean underwear was essential to self-respect, and she had often exhorted me to change my pants and vest regularly in case I got run over! I, being an ordinary East End kid, seemed always to have dirty underwear and only decided to change it when my mum spotted it and almost prised it off me. As it happened, on the day I had my accident, my underwear had been dirty but not filthy.

I strolled into the ward I had left only a week earlier, with my Wyatt Earp cap gun in one hand, and my Lone Star gun (with bullets) in the other.

One or two of the kids were still the same and I settled back into the routine quite easily.

Christmas in hospital was a happy affair. Visiting time was all day, and on Christmas Eve Father Christmas came into the hall downstairs on a porter's trolley pulled by five men. All the children got a present from the hospital, which I thought was fantastic. I received a game called "Cannon Ball" which was based on a television programme about a steam engine in the Wild West.

My parents brought from home all my Christmas presents, plus a few extra ones which neighbours had given Mum for me. I had a mass of toys and had a job selecting which special ones I wanted to keep with me. I wish, however that I had managed to keep more in the hospital ward, as that night, while my father was at work on his job as a night watchman, his car was stolen, and inside were all my presents. Needless to say, when the car was found, my presents were not.

My stay in the ward this time was to last several months. I was being treated with Cortisone, which began to have serious side-effects, so that my weight increased from five and a half stone, to over nine stone in eight weeks. I remember seeing myself in a mirror and thinking how much like Billy Bunter I looked. The drug gave me an insatiable appetite, and it was nothing for my parents and grandparents to bring eight large corned-beef sandwiches and half a chicken with them when they visited me. I used also to have masses of sweets, which I was supposed to hand in and share. But I used to hand half in and then secrete the rest under my mattress, in the back of my locker, under the fish tank or in the play room.

The time soon came for an important decision to be made.

Either I could continue taking the tablets and suffer the consequences of gross obesity, or reduce the tablets and virtually surrender any chance of regaining my former level of sight. The decision must have been difficult both for the doctors and for my parents, but it was finally decided to reduce the steroids and put me on a diet.

During this long period in hospital I was obviously missing my schooling, and it was decided to engage a home teacher for me. This "special" attention I enjoyed, and looked forward to Mrs. King coming to the hospital for lessons far more than I had ever looked forward to going to school.

Around this time too I became aware of just how much my eyesight had deteriorated. I could no longer read print, see the faces of people or recognise their features from more than a few feet. Yet despite these problems I still felt happy and cheerful. Every day seemed to provide new experiences and challenges and I do not remember feeling depressed or having any real sense of loss.

Towards the end of my stay in Moorfields I had a long discussion with my mum about the future. It was a conversation which she obviously found difficult. It must have been extremely painful for her to admit to herself that I would probably never see normally again, and to try to put it into terms a ten-year-old boy would understand, must have involved an unimaginable effort. Looking back now, she earns my admiration for having nevertheless done a good job. My damaged sight meant, first, a change of school, but my mother made this seem quite natural. The school was the Ryder School for the Partially Sighted, and as it happened I already knew a boy who attended it, as he lived opposite us. He did not seem "specially different" to me, except for the fact that he was taken to school in a big green coach; and this was a plus factor in any case as nobody else went to school in this way.

Two major problems on my discharge from hospital were, one, my immense size: (I was still over nine stone, and only 4 feet 6 inches tall),

And, two, I had a detached retina, which prevented me from doing any active sport. In fact my huge size probably saved my sight for a few months, as I doubt very much whether I would have been able to resist football or swimming if I had been physically fit enough to participate in them.

After the Easter holidays I was duly collected about 8.00 a.m. in the big green school bus. The attendant welcomed me and I was allocated a seat. The bus went through the East End of London, picking up about fifteen other children, and we arrived at the school at about nine.

My first impression of strangeness was that there were far fewer kids than I had been used to, most of them wearing glasses. I had never seen so many "four-eyed" kids in my life. The classes had only ten to fifteen pupils in each, whilst I had previously been in a class of forty-one.

Despite the small classes, however, I was surprised to find that the lessons were very much easier than those I had been used to, even though the classmates I was put with, were two or three years older than I was. Some of the mathematics we were asked to tackle as "advanced", I had covered during my last year at junior school. There was a general air of informality, and lessons were conducted in such a leisurely fashion that sometimes only four subjects were covered in a whole day. The headmaster seemed always to have pupils strolling into his office, and it soon became apparent that if you did not want to go to a particular lesson you could easily walk into Mr. Summers' office, engage him in conversation about the war, and then settle back to at least an hour of reminiscences, chocolate biscuits and sometimes a cup of tea! When you were eventually dismissed, because a visitor came or the phone rang, it was easy to return to class and say "the head master kept me".

In sport too I found differences. I was introduced to new games such as Spry and Corner Spry which I had never heard of. Spry was played by a team of people standing in a line with one player facing them on a centre spot. This player then threw a football to each of those in the line, and then changed places with the last person. The winners in any team competition were the team who finished first; that is, when each team member had performed the role of thrower. I found very quickly that although the game looked simple, it demanded pretty quick reactions and my sight level proved inadequate to follow the ball in the air with sufficient speed. I was eventually therefore relegated to the role of spectator.

Another sport that was new to me was known as "throwing the cricket ball". This was a version of putting the shot. I proved to be reasonably good at this (provided I was pointed in the right direction to throw the ball and didn't have to find it once I had done so). I was picked to represent the school in this event at the partially sighted sports day, and achieved the distinction of winning.

My stay at Ryder school was, however, brief, as it soon became clear to my teachers, my parents and myself that my sight level was not sufficient to cope there.

An appointment was made for me to see an ophthalmologist at County Hall who, after a thorough examination, confirmed all of our suspicions by finding that my sight was less than 3/60 of normal vision. The fraction of 3/60ths is a very important one, I have since learned, because it represents the dividing line between being registered as "partially sighted" or as "blind".

I had a struggle coming to terms with the idea of being "blind". I could not be blind! I could see. Tim, the boy in the hospital, was blind. He could not see at all. I did not want to be called blind, everyone felt sorry for blind people. If it came to that, I felt sorry for blind people myself. They were people, less fortunate than ourselves, whom you helped across the road whether they wanted to cross or not. They were people who used lovely dogs to walk around the streets with, or used thin metal canes with which they hit the walls or passers-by. They were blind, not me.

The length of time between my accident and my registration as blind 'had been no more than eight months. During this period, from a normal healthy ten-year-old boy with perfect vision, attending an ordinary school, I had become an eleven-year-old blind boy who had had five months off school and three months at a strange school at which he never settled, and was now faced with the prospect of having to leave home for a boarding school on the other side of London.

Yet, looking back, what strikes me now is that I accepted these things without ever feeling bitter or resentful. I do not even remember feeling frightened. Everything that happened seemed simply to be the next part of my life, and the fact that I had had an accident with a firework was almost irrelevant. I see now that my sense of "normality" was largely due to the almost super-human effort made by my mother. It was she who had the worries, and it was she who did the crystal ball gazing anticipating the future on my behalf. She had to make the biggest adjustments in her expectations, and to fight for the best chances for me. My accident may well have changed my life, but it shattered my mother's.

Mike, aged four, pageboy
at a cousin's wedding

Mike aged eight

I was born in the Hackney Hospital on 19th June 1950. I say in the hospital, but I should have added "only just".

My mother, nine months pregnant, had decided to go and do a little shopping on her own, so she got on the bus, and after about five minutes went into labour. The bus crew, no doubt alarmed but endeavouring to live up to London Transport's claim to offer service to customers, decided that there was no time to send for an ambulance and proceeded to drive the bus straight into the hospital forecourt. My mother then got off and walked into the maternity ward.

As a young child I apparently contracted and survived the usual range of children's illnesses. I had a seemingly endless capacity for getting myself dirty and was for ever being washed and changed. It was not my fault that my friends and I used to hold our Cowboy-and-Indian club meetings in the coal bunker.

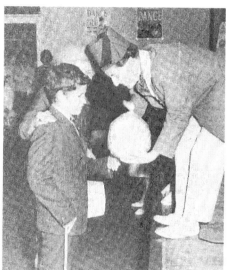

Mike at holiday camp aged 12

Our house was a large Victorian building in Stoke Newington. The top half was let out as a flat, and my family, which comprised my mother, father, Aunt Mary and brother John, lived in the bottom half. My mum worked as a manageress in a local shoe factory, and my father was also employed in the shoe industry as a night watchman. My aunt, I was told, was "slightly backward" and had lived with us ever since I could remember.

My mum, being the major bread-winner, had to go out to work; but she realised how important it was for my brother and me to have someone in the house when we came home from school. My Aunt Mary met this need wonderfully, and John and I certainly felt that we had the best of both worlds, in that we had virtually two mums.

I started school at Fleetwood Primary the term before my fifth birthday. I can remember the school very clearly. I did reasonably well in learning to read and write, and enjoyed art and P.E. but most of all I enjoyed sport. Sport was a very important part of the school's prestige, because it was through the football team that we competed with the children at other schools. So there was a great deal of rivalry for places in the first team. It was a proud day when I not only got in the team but was actually elected captain, and although under my captaincy we hardly won a game, I can still recall the wonderful feeling of elation I had when running on to the pitch at the head of my team.

I also played cricket, but with slightly less distinction. Whilst being one of the best bowlers in the side, I was undoubtedly the worst batsman and also a very unreliable fielder. I always had a fear when batting or fielding that the ball would hit me on the head, so used to shut my eyes whenever it came in my direction. My bowling however kept me in the side, and I was eventually found a place to field on the boundary.

I truanted occasionally, to go fishing, roaming over the park or swimming, but on the whole my attendance was good. I had a large group of friends, mostly centred on sport, and had a variety of interests ranging from collecting stamps and cigarette cards, to fishing and doing Airfix modelling. During the weeks at school I was always to be found where a ball was being kicked or hit. I would frequently arrive an hour early in the morning for a game of football in the playground, and would invariably stay behind for an hour in the evenings for more football.

On Saturdays I had a fixed routine: Saturday morning cinema club and then a trip down to Tottenham Hotspur's ground for the match—first team or reserve. I rarely missed a home match, unless sick or on holiday, and eventually came to be known by both officials and players. I had every Spurs team member's autograph and some of the players even knew me by name.

My visits to Spurs were initially in the company of my brother John, who was five years older than me, a good football player himself. He too had gone to Fleetwood and was remembered by many of the teachers.

At home my mother operated an open- door policy where friends were concerned. Most days there were my brother's or my own friends in, or friends calling for us to go out. So life on the whole was extremely happy, and very little happened to disturb our cosy existence.

Then, and I shall never know how much the accident affected it, my mother and father's relationship/marriage broke down. My mother later reassured me that the roots of the trouble went much further back than my accident!

Chapter 2

Partial Adjustments

Disability affects everyone within a family, not just the individual who is, or becomes, disabled, and in later years I was to understand more fully how the key to dealing with disability is in the strength the whole family can draw on from each other through the crisis. It is during the period of adjustment to disability that family members need each other most, and when outside support can be most useful. But in the early 1960s there were few community services available, and my mother found herself coping on her own, especially as my father came to withdraw from family involvement. For my part, I had to deal with entry into a boarding-school and separation from home and family at a time when I needed them most.

My first day at Linden Lodge School for the Blind was nerve-racking. First I remember being guided around the school by a very strange boy indeed. He not only looked odd but spoke in an unnatural high- pitched voice. I was shown my bed in the dormitory, which was a large room with thirteen beds in it. Up until that time, I had never been away from home on my own except in hospital, and certainly had never slept in such a large room with so many people. And I was in for another shock when I saw my classroom. The numbers in the class were even smaller than in the "partially sighted" school, and whereas there I had been struck by so many "four-eyed" kids, I was now horrified to learn that some of my new classmates had no eyes at all. I was also upset by the many mannerisms displayed by the other children. Some rocked violently, others sat with their fingers and knuckles poked in their eyes. One girl made peculiar gurgling noises, punctuated by occasional hoots. I remember thinking quite clearly that I would not stay with a load of loonies, and determining either to run away, or to get my mother to take me away at the earliest possible moment.

After a few days, however, I learned that I was only in this class to learn braille, and that when I had mastered it I would move up into the scholarship class. Re-learning the basic skills of reading and writing was certainly not easy. My lessons in braille started almost the first day, and I thought that I would never be able to memorise all the different combinations of the dots well enough to read and write braille other than at a snail's pace. I am not sure whether the credit was due to my discomfort and horror at my classmates, or to my high degree of intelligence (which had not hitherto been particularly in evidence), but I learned braille within eight weeks.

At the end of the eight weeks I moved into the scholarship class, and was relieved to find myself once again amongst fairly "normal" people who, apart from their lack of sight, appeared to be "like me". The purpose of the scholarship class was to coach the boys and girls in the class for the entrance examination to the two grammar schools for the blind, Worcester Grammar School for boys and Chorleywood for girls.

Three of us were to take the examination for Worcester in the following March, but the prospect of yet another change in my life, and the prospect of attending a school over 100 miles from London and my family, appalled me. This may have contributed to my lack of effort when it came to studying for the exam. I failed, which meant that I would stay at Linden Lodge, where academic opportunities were undeniably limited.

My mastery of braille did mean, however, that for the first time since my accident some twelve months earlier, I was able to read and write for myself. This achievement gave me immense pleasure and satisfaction, and I remember getting my first book out of the library and vowing that I would read it to 'the end even if it killed me.

Once able to read and write again, I could be included in lessons on other subjects. Some subjects were completely new to me and others, which I had studied at my sighted school, had a new look about them. Mathematics for example was performed by means of a metal board with hundreds of ten sided holes in it. Into these holes were placed small pieces of lead known as "types". At one end of the type were two dots and at the other a thin raised bar. The direction in which the bar or two dots pointed distinguished the number or process required. Using the frame and types was extremely cumbersome, especially to someone like myself who was not accustomed to using fine finger movements. The method also had no means of showing the working out of a problem, so that the student could not be told where in the sum he had gone wrong. Towards the end of my time at school, the frame was phased out and a method of writing down mathematical problems on a braille machine was devised.

Geography too was a problem. Whereas the sighted can look at a map of Europe, and take in main features at a glance, mapping by touch is very laborious. Different features of the country or continent can be represented in different textured plastic—for example, mountains raised and rough to the touch, rivers smooth and flat, areas within national boundaries speckled. But these maps are extremely difficult to understand, and were, I feel, the main cause of my giving up geography at a very early age.

Drawing and painting, which I had enjoyed at my sighted school, were replaced by woodwork and pottery, both of which I liked but never achieved much with. We always seemed to be making things for school fetes and I recall helping to produce tiles for table tops as though on a production line.

Religious Education too was a subject which acquired new dimensions. At school in the East End all religion had meant to me was a hymn and a prayer in assembly, and the children's broadcasts about Jesus once a week on a Friday. I had been expelled from the local Sunday school for misbehaviour (having stuffed a big bass drum stick down the cornet of the leader of our local Salvation Army band). At my new school, religion was a "subject". Assemblies lasted nearly half an hour, involving two or three hymns, Bible readings and a service over the radio. Even hymn singing involved preparation. At my sighted school we each had a hymn book to which the headmistress would ask us to refer. But at the blind school it was virtually impossible to read the words in braille and sing them at the same time, so all hymns had to be learned by heart. Most mornings we would go through the words of a well-known hymn line by line until we had learned them properly. The music master (who was blind himself) flew into a rage when we would not sing. When he was on his own we used to take advantage of his lack of sight to get up to mischief. I was frequently guilty of reading a book or playing cards, or simply acting the fool, flicking paper pellets, walking round the room or trying to get as close to the master without him realising I was there. I was caught on several occasions, but having reasonably quick wits I could usually think up some excuse for being out of my seat.

I started to learn typing, which, like mastering braille, was a major accomplishment, since it meant that I could now correspond with my sighted family and friends in a form which they could understand. I could write letters for myself, and no longer had to rely on other people to write them for me. This step towards independence may have been a small one, but it meant a lot to me at the time. Later, when I had girlfriends, the typing skill acquired even greater importance, since it meant I could write to them without having to endure the embarrassment of asking someone else to write my love letters.

Some subjects at school were noticeable by their absence, particularly biology and science. These were not included on the curriculum, either because there was no teacher to teach them, or because practical experiments would have been difficult to carry out by touch.

The greatest overall difference in all subjects was in the manner of teaching. At my sighted school nearly all the teachers had made use of the blackboard, and also, increasingly during the last years at my junior school, of visual aids such as slides, films and pamphlets. When school radio broadcasts were used, it was in conjunction with brightly coloured illustrated pamphlets. The theory was that visual aids helped to maintain interest in the subject, and that appeal to more than one of the senses enabled one to retain more information. In the blind school, however, there were no blackboards and everything had to be orally described. This was partly because there were inadequate books available in braille for most subjects. In any case, many of the pupils could not read braille fluently enough to be able to understand what they read, let alone convey it to the rest of the class.

The problem in reading braille is that the inherent slowness of the process makes it much more difficult than in reading ordinary type to remember what one has read a few sentences or paragraphs back, so that to follow an argument over any large body of text takes an extraordinary effort of concentration.

I found then, as now, that the lack of visual stimulation when studying diminished my ability to concentrate and reduced the amount of subject matter I retained. I began to drop off to sleep during lessons, not because I was tired but because I was bored.

The only subject that did not seem to change much was P.E. It was very similar to the sort of thing I had been doing in my sighted school. We did exercises, running, football and cricket and

I think during my time at school it was the only lesson for which I was never late.

Two subjects which did have a great effect on my life were music and drama. For introducing me to music in particular I shall always be grateful to that school. We had the opportunity of studying not only classical music, but popular music too. I was given the opportunity of learning to play a whole variety of instruments, ranging from piano and organ to drums, guitar, double bass and clarinet. I took up the clarinet and surprised myself by managing to play it reasonably well. My enthusiasm for classical music however diminished when "musical appreciation" was included as a compulsory subject in the evenings. I objected most strongly at being required to study in what I regarded as my free time. Although I had a vivid imagination I could not, at the age of twelve, imagine fairies dancing across the hillside when the flute was played. When sitting in a hot stuffy room listening to classical pieces, all I appreciated was that I was inside instead of outdoors playing football, so the classes acted rather like aversion-therapy. To this day I have never been able to sit and listen to classical music with enjoyment. The lesson did however have its bright side, because it was taken by the blind music master and more often than not I was able to find my own relief by listening to the radio through an ear-piece or displaying my unrivalled talent for making paper aeroplanes. I also used these sessions to teach other boys how to play cards.

My enthusiasm was really fired up, however, when I discovered folk music. One of the teachers taught guitar, and soon three other boys and I had formed a folk group and were spending many happy hours practising songs and giving concerts. Folk music provided me with my first real hobby since having to give up stamp collecting, and the group was really very good. We were soon asked to play for visitors in school, and in due course built up quite a following in hospitals, old people's homes and other schools. At one point we even appeared on television on the "Songs of Praise" programme.

The group provided me with an opportunity for building and testing my own self-confidence. For the first time since becoming blind, I had to get up in front of people and perform. At first I was extremely nervous and found it difficult to look out at an audience whom I could not see but who could see me. But the confidence gained at that early stage of blindness is something that has stood me in good stead ever since, both in my sporting activities and in my career as a social worker.

Drama, too, did a great deal to boost my morale. It was the headmaster's pet subject, and not only was it included in the school curriculum, but sometimes, when one of his "productions" was in rehearsal, it took precedence over everything else. I sometimes wondered whether, if as much effort had been put into some of the other subjects, more children would have emerged with a better general education. But these extravaganzas were extremely well acted and produced. In the weeks immediately prior to a performance academic work would virtually stop, and the educational production line would be switched to the manufacturing of paper flowers, scenery or costumes. The paper flowers I remember very well: they appeared at every lesson, from maths and geography to R.E.; and we were told that we could make the flowers while we listened to the teacher. Even in the evenings our labours were not at an end, as we had to scour the neighbourhood selling tickets for the play. I am sure the people living near the school used to dread our annual performances. They must have known the sales routine as well as we did—knock knock, "Good evening, would you like to buy a ticket for our school's latest production of... Tickets are 50p each and refreshments are available". Many used to buy tickets to get us off their doorsteps, others both bought tickets and came out of curiosity; and some actually enjoyed the plays.

For us, the performances generated a wealth of material for laughter, especially when things went wrong. On one occasion I had been responsible for recording the bubble sound effects for the cauldron in the witches' scene in Macbeth. I had recorded the noise on a small tape recorder, which was secreted in the pot. My bubbles and the carbon ice to make the steam worked extremely well and everyone was pleased. Unfortunately, at the end of the scene the props remover forgot to turn the tape off, and throughout the whole of the next act gurgling and bubbling noises could be heard belching out of the wings!

The plays were designed not only to give us self-confidence, but also to help with general mobility. You had to learn to walk across the stage, and to orientate yourself in relation to the other players and to the props. On one occasion the orientation of one of the boys went a little wrong, and instead of walking off the stage he strolled straight into the chair-store at the back, which, as the play was about sailors, was being used as the captain's cabin. All would have been well, if the boy, believing he was out of sight of the audience, had not proceeded to pick his nose with great gusto. His antics got a bigger laugh than the dialogue on stage.

Another incident that caused me some embarrassment took place during our school's presentation of Androcles and the Lion. I played the Roman centurion and was dressed in a skirt- type tunic. At one point I had to sit on a grassy bank and talk to the Christians. Unfortunately, the person making the bank had put the bolsters under the green canvas too close together and had left no room for me to sit down. Accordingly, when I lowered my behind I slid off the bank and fell over backwards, causing my skirt to fly up over my head and treat the audience to an unobstructed view of my bright blue pants.

No strangeness in my new school life, however, was to be compared with the differences in my domestic and social life. I found it extremely difficult to get used to life in a dormitory with thirteen other boys, each of us with only a small locker in which to keep our personal possessions and a chair to put our clothes on. The beds were metal framed and the mattresses extremely hard, most of them packed with horsehair or straw. At a time in my life when privacy had begun to be important to me, I was plunged into an environment where privacy did not exist. Not only was I expected to sleep in the same room as others, but I also had to bath with them, sometimes actually in somebody else's dirty water! I was not too fond of water at the best of times, and total immersion in water was something I left strictly to the Baptists. In my house in Hackney we did not have a bathroom, and we bathed in an old tin bath in front of the fire. As the preparation of the bath meant a great deal of effort, it did not take too many protestations on my part to convince my family that they should abandon the idea and leave me to have a strip-wash instead. Now I was expected to have a bath every day whether I was dirty or not. And as if the dreaded water torture were not enough shock in itself, I had to get used to the fact that all bathing was supervised by women members of the staff! By the time I went to the blind school I had already reached the stage of being embarrassed to bath in front of my mum, let alone anyone else, and the thought of a stranger seeing my private parts caused me real misery. The bathing lady obviously thought nothing of it, and so did most of the other boys: boys of twelve and thirteen would quite happily stand around with nothing on, talking about the latest episode of "Dr Who" while wiping their earholes out with a flannel. Nobody seemed to observe my embarrassment. After a time, however, I became less self-conscious and was eventually able to talk about "Dr Who" and clean my earholes out as naked as the rest of them.

The daily domestic routine appeared to me so strictly regimented as virtually to eliminate any need to think for oneself at all. We had set times to get up, set times to eat, set times to clean our shoes, set ways to make our beds, set days to change the sheets, set days to change our pants, set times to go to bed, and set times for lights out. For blind children, whose problem in later life would be to gain and retain as much independence as possible, the clockwork regime experienced at the school would prove to be a calamity. Becoming institutionalised significantly reduced the ability of many of us to function independently, and certainly created problems for some of us on leaving school. Everything was provided for us, we were not encouraged to learn the value of anything, or to take responsibility for the care of what we wore or used. Clothing and school equipment became expendable: if one ripped one's trousers or kicked the toes of one's shoes out they were only the school's and would be replaced.

Everyone had to wear school uniform, except on those weekends when we went home, or on special expeditions out of the school. The argument was that this was fairest to those children whose parents could not afford smart clothes. So the boys had to put up with hideous grey trousers and enormous beetle-crusher shoes which were only one step removed from navvy boots, instead of the winkle pickers or chisel toes and coloured shirts that our peers were wearing. We already felt different being blind, without emphasising our differences with "prison uniforms" as we called them. I remember once hearing someone in the street say as we passed "It's those blind children from the orphanage".

Yet, looking back, I realise that in spite of the strangeness of it all I settled in remarkably quickly. I liked the company of the other boys most of the time, and enjoyed always having someone available, and willing to play with me. I was able to rediscover sport, albeit in an adapted form, and the other lads in the dormitory certainly helped me a great deal with my braille. In the evenings some of the senior boys made up their own 'radio' programmes on tape, which they broadcast over the school's speaker system, and I was soon asked to contribute to these. One boy taught me how to play chess, and we would play until one or two o'clock in the morning. We used to place the chessboard on the chair between our two beds, neither of us of course bothered about when the lights went out. The "blind" chessboard is made with the black squares raised, and each square has a hole drilled in the middle of it. On the bottom of each piece there is a spike which fits into the holes in the board. One can tell which piece is which by the shape, and on the top of all the white pieces a small point distinguishes it from the black ones. The blind chess player is thus able to feel the positions of his own and his opponent's pieces without dislodging them.

The other boys in the dormitory did not altogether appreciate our pastime, complaining that they were being woken up by the sound of fingers groping over the pieces and rattling them as they worked out the next move. But they had their own back one memorable morning, when my friend forgot that the board was on the chair and sat down to put his socks on. As his naked posterior alighted on the white chess pieces he let out an ear-piercing scream and shot to his feet, while we recognised the sound of chess pieces dropping from where they had become embedded in his behind.

Even our evenings were organised for us, and we had no choice about attending activities such as dancing, sport or Scouts. The inclusion of economics and the dreaded musical appreciation as "leisure activities" was difficult to bear gracefully. At one time the headmaster had the brilliant idea of sending us running around the grounds at 7.30 every morning regardless of the weather. I argued strongly that if we were at home, we would not have been forced into doing this, and therefore we should not be forced to do it at school. Luckily the headmaster's enthusiasm for this running idea lasted only one day, and it was dropped.

The other problem I had with all this "organisation" was in finding time and space to be alone. We slept, ate and socialised with the same people all week. The grounds of the school were so small, and the timetable so full, that we had little chance to be alone and think, read, or just day-dream. I remember longing sometimes for solitude, but rarely achieving it.

I did however forge strong links with many of the staff, some of whom I have kept in touch with ever since. One of the housemothers, for instance, Miss Lake, provided much of the mothering I missed by being at boarding school. She was warm and kind and always ready for a laugh. I used to enjoy being sick and having to stay in bed, as Miss Lake would bring me tea or sit and chat for a while. Barbara, another house matron, was more like a big sister and she was also great fun. I took the mickey out of her relentlessly, but she always responded in good humour. Both matrons I have kept in touch with since leaving school, and Barbara eventually married one of my friends.

Barry, one of the housefathers, took me and a couple of other boys under his wing. He involved us in a great many activities, including boating on the Norfolk Broads, and camping. He was one of the few teachers who actually treated us as though we were reasonably normal human beings! Barry talked to me about the things that I, as an adolescent, most wanted to know about girls and work, and he encouraged me to try new things. His friend Bill Aitken, one of the teachers, also provided me with much needed family links and contacts. I suppose, looking back, that Bill constituted a kind of substitute father for me—someone I respected, liked and enjoyed being with. He and his wife and children encouraged the boys to drop in at their home, and I shall never forget the pleasure I had of sitting in his front room listening to his records, or singing while he played the guitar or accordion.

The fact that for the first eleven months after the accident I still had some limited vision, I was able to adjust to my blindness by degrees. I was able to get used to coping with less sight, and to begin developing my other senses of touch, taste and smell. Even after I went to Linden Lodge I was still doing things 'visually", that is, using vision as my primary orientation. I looked where I was going and did not need to use a white stick. I could still recognise people if they stood close enough to me. When I was at home, I was still able to play the same type of games as before with my sighted friends—I even continued to ride my bike in the street, much to the horror of my mother. I found however that gradually I had to rely on hearing more, and I learned to discriminate more and more finely between sounds so that I could hazard a guess at what was outside my field of vision. Crossing roads, for example became an increasingly difficult and dangerous business, and I had to learn both to listen and to look, and to cross only when both senses were satisfied that the road was clear.

Even during my first year at the blind school, I had some residual sight which made my adjustment easier. I could orientate myself within the school buildings and the school grounds, even though these were at least twenty times larger than my East End school and its playground. I felt more fortunate than my totally blind classmates, and when I read in a book that "In the land of the blind the one-eyed man is king", I remember feeling grateful that the one-eyed man was me.

But I knew that my remaining sight was fragile, and soon I was called upon to make some momentous decisions.

The first decision arose over the partially detached retina in my left eye. This, I was told, precluded me from doing any sport in case I banged my head and detached the retina completely. For the first fifteen months or so I did as I was told and took no part in any physical activities. This was no particular hardship at the time because due to my Cortisone treatment I was four stone overweight and had no desire to do anything energetic. However, as my body weight returned to its proper level and the opportunities for sport increased, I became more and more anxious to join in. The thought of being totally inactive, perhaps for the rest of my life, was almost unbearable and during one of my many trips to Moorfields for a check-up I asked the doctors just what the alternatives were. The doctor put them in very simple terms that even I, aged eleven-and-half, could understand: either I refrained from doing any physical activity which might result in my jerking or knocking my head, or I could lead a normal life and take my chances.

Age 14 with friend Alan on a journey to Paris

Mike, with his friend Chris, about eight months after going blind

My mother and I talked the matter over at great length. Eventually we agreed that, as living the life of a statue was neither in my nature nor guaranteed to retain the little sight I had, I would, from that moment on, join in anything I wanted, within reason, and begin to live life to the full again. Once the decision was made it did not take me too long to be selected for the school football team and to involve myself in virtually every sporting activity going.

The second big decision arose when my right eye began to give me a great deal of pain. This eye, had not been damaged by the blast of the bottle, and for a few weeks after the accident I had had perfect sight in it. But it later developed a strange condition whereby, in effect, it decided to go on strike in sympathy with my left eye. I therefore had only a limited amount of sight in both eyes. But one morning I awoke with an excruciating pain in my right eye. My mother took me to the hospital, but although various eye drops and ointments were tried, the pain did not diminish. If anything it got worse. I found that (the only thing that soothed it, was to bathe the eye constantly in cold water, so for several days I carried a cup of cold water and a pad of cotton-wool everywhere I went. It was obvious that something had to be done, and when I became feverish the hospital decided to admit me and put me under sedation.

During the next two days my mother had a series of consultations with the doctors. When she finally told me the outcome of their deliberations I could tell from her face that the news was not good. Near to tears, she said that there were two options for relieving the pain, both of which were unpleasant: I could either have the eye taken out completely, or have it injected to reduce the pressure. The second option appeared to be the obvious one, until I was told that not only would it virtually put paid to any hope of seeing out of that eye again, but also I had to be conscious when they injected it. At that moment, I certainly knew what the expression "between the devil and the deep blue sea" meant. I decided finally that while my eye was my own there was some hope, and I chose to have the injection. It is sufficient to say that the injection was every bit as painful as I imagined it would be. I had to have four nurses holding me down in case I jumped, and I was told that my scream stopped the buses in the High Street. The worst moment of all was seeing with my left eye the needle pass by my nose on its way into my right eye. Luckily however pain passes, and the memory of it fades. The injection relieved the pressure and stopped the pain in the eye. After two weeks or so I was able to go back to school, able to see only with one eye but still able to see.

Chapter 3

Totally Blind

When at last I did lose my sight completely, it was, ironically, not because I was playing a rough game but because I was playing the passive role the doctors had advised. I was unable to play football that day, for one reason or another, and had been relegated to the role of supporter in a match against a local Boys' Club. I had managed to borrow a bugle, which I blew with much vigour to cheer our side on. We won the match and that evening I went to bed happy. The next day being Friday, I went home, not noticing that there was anything wrong with my sight. But on the Saturday morning when I awoke, I could see nothing, and just lay there rigid. I closed my eyes and opened them again, half believing that perhaps I was still asleep. I could still see nothing.

I managed to get up and dress myself. I shuffled out to the stairway feeling with my feet for the steps and groping with my hands for the banister. On reaching the ground floor I called for my mother, and said that I thought we had better go to the hospital as something had gone wrong with my eyes. I then remembered that Mum was at work and asked my dad what we should do. We agreed to see how things developed during the day, and if my sight did not return, go to the hospital that night or the following morning. During the day some of my sight returned but in a very misty, hazy form.

Most of that day I spent sitting in an armchair or fiddling with a bell I was trying to wire up for my bedroom. I wanted to do something to take my mind off what I feared was happening, but I found I could not concentrate on anything. When my mother came home from work I told her what had happened and we agreed to go to the hospital the following morning. We kidded ourselves that "perhaps I had a cold in the eye", but deep down I think we both knew that it was much more than that.

When I awoke the following morning the mistiness of the previous day had gone and in its place was total blackness. We went to the hospital and the doctors confirmed our suspicions.

In some sense I was actually relieved, for the worst that could happen had happened and the threat of becoming totally blind no longer hung over me like a dark cloud. My retina had detached itself further and there was no possibility of operating as I had also had a massive haemorrhage behind the eye. The doctor thought that almost certainly the pressure I had used to blow the bugle had caused the haemorrhage. I was admitted immediately and told to lie still and rest. Pads were put on my eyes, and I found myself in almost the identical position 1 had been in two years earlier when I had had my accident. This time however, I did know what lay in store for me, and my feelings were very different. Nothing I could do could stop me worrying about whether I would be able to cope with life as a totally blind person. I was like Tim, the boy I had admired so. I was blind. I remember feeling terrified, angry and anxious. Would I be able to cope as well as Tim and the boys at school? I finally resolved that if they had managed, so should I.

At the same time as these feelings were going through my mind I was very conscious of having to put on a brave face for my mother's sake, who had obviously taken my total loss of sight badly. Yet she did not break down and weep all over me (something that would have upset me greatly), but tried to look at things practically and carry on as normally as possible, to give me strength. My Uncle Bill also played an important part in helping me to accept my new state. He used to come into the hospital and play cards with me every afternoon without fail. He was always funny and never failed to make me laugh, even when I was feeling down. He would teach me new card games and sit for hours playing brag or cribbage for pennies. His visits I looked forward to immensely, and the closeness to him and fondness for him that I developed at that time have remained with me today. He was an extremely important person to me when I most needed important people.

My father came less often to see me, only partly because his job as a night watchman prevented him. I had found it more and more difficult to talk to him since my accident, and seemed to see him less often when I was at home at weekends or holidays. I knew that he and Mum were not getting on well together, and it did not come as a shattering surprise when my mum said that she and Dad were going to live apart for a while to "see how things went". So Dad went to live with my Nan and I visited him and Nan there from time to time, which I quite enjoyed as I was the focus of attention. Mum and Dad decided eventually to make the split permanent and divorce proceedings were started. I remember being concerned that my friends at school should not know what had happened at home, so when I was asked why my Dad didn't pick me up any more on Fridays I merely said that he was working. But I honestly don't remember going through any of the pain and anguish which usually accompanies parental break-up. I suppose I was too busy coping with my own emotional and practical problems.

I realised that I had already made many adjustments during the time I had had partial sight, and had achieved a degree of self-confidence and independence, and most importantly a strong will to tackle problems and overcome them. My strong will, independence and ability to rise to a challenge, were characteristics of my personality that would be needed even more in the future. My strong will in particular, was to help me cope with the many frustrations of total blindness.

The sudden transition from partial to total blindness made it necessary to relearn virtually everything that I had done previously by sight. I had, for example, to learn how to recognise the difference between items of my clothing; which shirt was which, for example, and if possible what colours they were. It took me several weeks to master tying my shoe laces without looking at my feet, and making my bed without leaving creases in it or bits of blanket sticking out. I 'had to overcome the intricate difficulty of squeezing toothpaste on to the toothbrush—I frequently ended up using half a tube a week, before I learned to put more paste on the bristles than on the washbasin. And I had to get used to using my hands and feet to feel where I was walking. Later I learned how to get around using a white stick, and gained enough confidence to tackle public transport; but in those early months I fell down many stairs and tripped over endless objects.

At mealtimes, I had to learn to recognise what I was eating by feeling it with my fork. I then had to master getting it on to the fork and finally conveying it from the plate to my mouth. At first it took me ages to fix the food on the fork. Then, having got the fork up to its goal, I would find that the food had dropped off or, worse still, that I didn't like what I was chewing. It was too late to spit it out and I had to grit my teeth and swallow. I must have eaten more empty ends of forks than most people have had hot dinners!

My mother played a very important part in this "relearning", not least because she never prevented me from trying new things, even if it meant taking risks. She allowed me for example to make tea for myself. Some of my attempts at independence did indeed end in disaster, as when I tried to press my own trousers. The iron was too hot, and instead of making a nice crease I managed to burn right through the tea towel and both legs of my trousers, leaving an iron-shaped hole through the lot.

As my other senses developed I learned to recognise what was happening by relating certain sounds to sighted memories. For example, one evening when I was at home with my mother and brother watching T.V. I remember hearing my brother clap his hands and say "thanks" as though he had caught something. By that sound alone, I could describe almost exactly what had happened. My mother had taken a cigarette out of a packet and held it up to my brother. He had nodded, and my mum had thrown it to him, and he had caught it. I had obviously seen that many times before, and now I was able to connect the actions with the sounds.

Also, my physical co-ordination improved and I was able to transfer something from one hand to the other without looking at what I was doing. I could put food in my mouth first time instead of spreading it over my face. Instinctive reactions I learned to control: for instance, I found out the hard way that I should bend my knees, and never to bend from the waist to pick up something I had dropped, as invariably there would be a corner of a table or the back of the chair just where my face came down. At one time I had so many scars on my forehead that it was impossible to see an unblemished bit of skin. My shins and legs also took a bashing before I learned not to move suddenly forward without checking whether the way was clear. During the first few weeks back at school after I became totally blind, my mother used to dread me coming home at weekends as she was frightened of what new injuries she would be confronted with. I remember telephoning her after one particularly nasty accident, when I had run into an iron bar and broken my nose. My face had so many cuts and scabs on it, I was certain that she would faint dead away, if she had no warning.

I had also to redevelop a sense of direction. In those early months I would frequently have to be rescued from the flower beds, or guided back from the middle of the lawn after spending hours wandering around in ever-decreasing circles. If I was late for a lesson the class would send a search party out for me. My love of P.E. and my workouts in the gymnasium helped a great deal to develop my orientation skills, and eventually I was taught to estimate where I was in relation to objects, and to orientate myself in relation to the long and short sides of the gymnasium when shooting a football. My sense of touch also improved and I became quite good at recognising most items by how they felt. Like a small baby, I soon learned that my tongue and lips were more sensitive than my hands and anything I did not recognise I put in my mouth.

As the months went by I also learned to listen to the TV and understand what was happening even though I could not see the action. Certain things of course I could not cope with: silent films for example were useless to me; and I remember staying up late one night to watch the midnight movie only to find that it was made in French with sub-titles.

I found that in addition to my own personal adjustments I had constantly to educate family and friends. My mother for example would come up to say goodnight, find I was reading my braille book, and leave the light on so that I could see, so nearly every night I would have to get out of bed and check whether the light switch was up or down. Similarly, when I was visiting relatives, they would rush to turn the light on in the toilet or on the stairs.

This failure of perception worked the other way too. I used to forget completely that because I could not see other people, it did not mean that other people could not see me. More often than not I would fail to pull the bedroom curtains before I undressed. Several old ladies in the flats opposite my window at school telephoned to complain about my acts of exhibitionism! I bet they enjoyed them really, and polished their binoculars every night!

Inevitably, my blindness brought with it a great deal of embarrassment which, although it seems funny now, upset me greatly at the time. I would sit down on a chair and find myself with the back of the chair at my side; or on the underground find myself back to elbow with the next passenger. I even sat once or twice on someone's lap, thinking the seat was empty; and once, as my piece de resistance, missed a chair completely and ended up sprawled on the floor. I would try to eat ice lollies with their wrappings on them, or pick up containers by the wrong end and spill their contents all over the floor of the shop. Other people would think it was funny if I happened to have odd socks on, but I did not.

But what disturbed me most of all was that people would talk about me in my hearing as if I was stupid. As I boarded a bus I could hear old women saying things like "Ain't it a shame, a good looking young boy too".

Strangers in the street would walk by and mutter "Poor little sod". Shopkeepers would ask my mother whether I liked sweets, and when we visited strangers she would really be asked the classic question "Does he take sugar". Even at twelve this insensitive behaviour made me angry, and I would upset my mum by replying with

"Well, if you asked him he might bloody well tell you".   .

One aunt was particularly embarrassing because she found it difficult to say the word "blind". So she adopted a form of sign language to let everyone know. I remember going into a shop with her when I could still see a little. As I asked for some sweets, I was conscious of the shopkeeper looking past me. I turned around suddenly and saw my aunt engaged in a complicated semaphore which reminded me of a tic-tac man at the race course. She was undoubtedly trying to convey the fact that I could not see, but I don't think the shopkeeper knew what was going on—he must have thought he had in his shop a female Magnus Pyke.

This aunt, took me out a great deal, thus relieving some of the pressure on my mother, obviously meant well, but she certainly enhanced rather than reduced the embarrassment that I experienced!

The total loss of my sight did bring with it for me a period of loneliness and depression, especially at home. As I could no longer play the type of games my sighted friends wanted to play, one by one they stopped calling until, at weekends and holidays, no friends called at all. Whereas I used to long for school to be over and the holidays or weekends to begin, now the reverse became true and the summer holidays in particular were endured rather than enjoyed. When events or visits were arranged at school in the weekends I used to choose to stay at school, unaware of the hurt this caused my mother, who did everything she could to alleviate my loneliness and boredom. She would read to me for hours, and arrange outings and trips whenever she could.

She realised that it was friends of my own that I most needed and longed for. So eventually she went to the length of asking someone she worked with to ask her son if he would come and "sit" with me. I was furious when she told me what she had done, but secretly I hoped that the boy would come and that we would become friends. The day of our meeting arrived, and I was surprised when Alan brought his friend Keith with him. Alan had brought him for moral support, as I think he found the prospect of visiting a blind boy as daunting as going to the dentist. Alan was shy and as embarrassed as I was, but I liked him immediately. Keith, by contrast, was very extrovert and throughout that first visit had Alan and me in stitches of laughter, which greatly helped to ease the underlying tension. Keith, for example, when he saw my braille cards, asked "What are those pinholes in the corners, do they help you cheat?"

All three of us became great friends, and virtually every weekend would meet up to do something. On Saturdays we played cards at the house of one of us, on Sundays we would go fishing or take a trip on the buses with Red-Rover tickets. Both of them treated me quite naturally and frequently forgot I was blind, to the extent of forgetting that I needed guiding, and would walk off without me. They would play mad games with me and have pillow fights. But when on our fishing trips or exploring, they would always help me to climb a bank or wade across a stream.

This normal treatment contrasted with what I was getting from my family, some of whom had begun to be very protective and to regard me as the family pet. Nothing I did was wrong, anything I wanted I could have. Though I liked being spoiled, of course, even this was confusing, because I was being treated as "different"— and I did not feel any different.

So Alan and Keith's friendship came at a time when I needed it most. I shall always be grateful to them for what they did for me, even though they were not necessarily conscious at the time of what it was they were doing. Their friendship made the weekends and the holidays enjoyable once again, and I was able to regard myself as very lucky in having sighted friends, because the majority of those at the blind school seemed to have no contact with people their own age at home.

Other more profound and subtle adjustments had also to be made. I had for the first time to get used to the fact that I was, and probably would be for the rest of my life, dependent on other people for things that I would ordinarily have done for myself. As a ten-year-old I had been reasonably self-reliant. Like other East End kids, I could travel on public transport on my own, could get a snack for myself if necessary and felt confident enough to go into a cafe alone to eat if I wanted to. Now that I was blind I had to rely on others to take me across roads, especially when it was raining, when the cars would not stop, passers-by had no time or did not notice that I needed help, and I was getting soaked. I knew, although I was encouraged to be as independent as possible, that this "independence" would always be limited and I found it very difficult to come to terms with the idea. I had also to learn always to accept help politely even when I did not need it, because if help was rejected (especially rudely) it might not be offered again on an occasion when it really was needed.

Aged 15, with a family group

As the years went by and my general mobility improved, the big day arrived when I was allowed out of the school on my own. I had to undergo a mobility course, involving a series of tests to prove to an examiner that I was competent to be let out without an escort. The first test was a walk round the block, the second test a bus journey, the third a bus and tube journey, and so on until eventually I had used all forms of public transport. There was no actual training available of how best to use my white stick, or in techniques for recognising places: these things I just had to find out for myself.

My first real journey was to travel home alone across London on a Friday afternoon. The journey involved a tube and bus ride and I accomplished it without very much difficulty, getting home before my mother returned from work and so saving her the anxious moments at the door suspecting the worst. On the

Sunday, however, I had to make the return journey, and all that day I was aware that my mum was anxious and worried. She offered to come back with me that night, but I said that I would like to do it on my own, and promised to ring her as soon as I got back to school. I set off to the sounds of "be careful" and "take care" and tapped off down the road, nervous but determined. The journey with my mother usually took about one and a half hours. That evening I did it in just on the hour. Even so, when I rang the telephone could only have rung once before my mother picked it up, and I could hear the relief when she heard my voice. I learned later that she had not left the seat by the telephone since I had left, and when she put the phone down she had to run shaking to the bathroom to be violently sick. This performance was repeated week after week until my mother was able to relax a little and her fear that "another" accident would happen to me faded.

My problems in accepting my lot were made worse in my middle teens by the onset of adolescence. At this time I began to doubt my own abilities, and my self-confidence dropped to its lowest level to date. I was full of doubt about whether I would ever meet members of the opposite sex, let alone whether I, a mere blindy, could possibly attract and keep a girlfriend. I was sure that no sighted girl would look at me when there were so many "normal" blokes around. What is more, sighted boys had cars or motor bikes, while all I could offer was an E-type white stick, and even that looked as though it could do with a respray. I was also acutely aware of those situations where I would have to rely on a girl to do things for me instead of vice versa. My role as male had to be completely rethought, since I could not possibly conform to the stereotype male who asserted himself in difficult situations, ordered the meals and generally took control.

My experience of girls by the age of sixteen had been very limited, and most of my dates had ended in disaster and embarrassment. I remember taking one girl out for the day, and doing quite well until the need arose to go to the toilet. The girl was obviously embarrassed at having not only to locate the Gents but to direct me once I was in. Having got over that, I decided to take her for something to eat, but all I managed to find open was a self-service cafe. She managed to load both trays quite well, but then she had to carry her tray and at the same time guide me carrying mine. We were both very conscious of people in the restaurant watching us, and I was upset not only on my own behalf but also on hers.

Even if I found a girl who would put up with these trials and tribulations, I used to wonder, how then could I take her home? I could just imagine kissing a girl goodnight on her doorstep and then asking her if she could walk me home, as I didn't know the way. Or, even worse, being found the following morning still stumbling round her front garden trying to find the gate!

My opportunities to meet girls of my own age were in any case very few. I was at boarding school all week, and at weekends I knew of no youth club that either could or would accept me as a member. The one weekend dance I plucked up courage to attend so humiliated me that I vowed never to go to a dance again. I had agreed to go with my two sighted friends, and as soon as we got there I knew that it was a mistake. Since I could not see where the girls were sitting I could not go up and ask them to dance. Propriety dictated that no girls would come and ask me to dance, and I refused, point blank, to allow my friends to go and ask a girl for me! Can you imagine the scene;

"Hallo luv, would you like to dance with my friend, he's blind but quite harmless".

We eventually worked out a system whereby I and one of my friends would go together up to two girls and ask them both to dance. This worked well enough, in that both girls accepted, but my problems were not over. Since the dancing was the kind that

46

demanded no physical contact with my partner, I found it difficult to work out where she was, and ended up either dancing with the person next to her or prancing about facing in the opposite direction. If I did manage to finish the dance without making a fool of myself, my partner would thank me and walk back to her seat, leaving me stranded in the middle of the floor looking like a goldfish that had just jumped out of its bowl. My friends would eventually have to abandon their own conquests to rescue me.

Mike Aged 16, on holiday with friends.

With Stepfather Ron on holiday aged 18

Even this occasion however, was less embarrassing than some of our social trips from school. Once, for instance, we had been invited to visit a local girls' school for the evening, and I had put on my best clothes and splashed the aftershave on all over as though it was going out of fashion. When we arrived, we were grouped with some of the girls from the hosting school and shown to some seats. When it came to sitting down and talking I was in my element. But as soon as the music started I knew I was on a loser. Wafts of lovely perfume were drifting up my nostrils and sending my vest whipping up my back like a roller blind. But the girls to whom I had been speaking were dancing and there seemed to be no partner for me. Then I was aware of a sweet-smelling creature sitting quietly next to me. Having first crossed my fingers I cleared my throat and said,

"Would you like to dance?"

My stomach turned over when I heard the voice of one of my friends:

"Sod off you idiot, it's me, Derek".

I managed to laugh it off and say something like "I knew it was you really, I was just joking", and prayed that he would not spread the story round the whole school and make me a laughing stock.

Although I later related these anecdotes with humour, I did not in fact feel at all happy or humorous at the time and resented my blindness bitterly for causing me such trauma. One day indeed I felt so low that for a split second I contemplated suicide. I was standing on the tube platform on my way home on a Friday, and I remember debating in my head whether to end it all and jump under the next train that came.

Nobody would miss me, I told myself, and my misery would be over. But the very thought that I could contemplate such a drastic action frightened me enough to pull me up short, and my moment of self-pity was over almost as quickly as I was aware of it. This moment of adolescent despair I have never been able to tell anyone about, and I feel sure that if I had done so at the time I would simply have been told not to be silly and to "cheer up". But it showed me that though I thought I had made a complete adjustment, the process, is continuous, and one never stops having to adapt.

My teenage anxieties also coincided with the dawning of more concrete concerns over my career prospects. I knew that I would need at least some qualifications for work, or further studies. But I was only too well aware that there were massive gaps in my general education, and that the subjects at which I was at 'O' level standard were very few.

"O" level English Literature and Language were exams that almost the whole of my class took, but a girl and I were also entered for a C.S.E. examination in Social Studies, and I was entered in a variety of Royal Society of Arts examinations. Typing was one, and I had shown some spark of ability in arithmetic, despite the difficulties of its performance, so arithmetic was another subject I took. Considering that, if I had not gone blind I would probably have gone to grammar school, and taken many "0" levels, these few examinations were certainly below my capabilities. Even taking these few exams, distinguished me, as the pupil who gained the most examinations, in the history of the school. I am pleased to say that I managed to pass them all except typing, and even managed to gain an O level grade in my C.S.E. Three "O" levels would not open up the world to me but they were still more than most of my classmates had.

The examinations brought with them thoughts of the future, and what work I would like to do. The idea of leaving my nice safe school environment to enter the nasty outside world frightened me. Everything, as I have said, was done for you at school, and the prospect of having to make my own decisions worried me. A school leavers' conference was arranged, and I knew I would be asked what I wanted to do, but the problem was that I didn't know. All the things I had ever wanted to be as a child were no longer possible; to my certain knowledge British Rail did not employ blind train drivers, and the Metropolitan Police were not recruiting blind policemen even for night duty in areas with no street lamps!

The range of options in fact open to me was very limited. They amounted to a choice between becoming a shorthand or audio-typist, a telephonist or a lathe operator. I did not have enough qualifications to consider either computer programming or physiotherapy.

At the leavers' conference, the headmaster and the representatives from the Royal National Institute for the Blind agreed that shorthand-typing was what I should think about, and offered to arrange an interview for me at a college in London which taught this subject to the blind. Since none of those advising seemed to have much idea of what a career as a shorthand-typist entailed, I was not convinced. The headmaster made no secret of his displeasure when I resisted this forecast for my future.

Eventually, however, I could come up with nothing better and so agreed to go for an interview at Pembridge Place Commercial College. I was offered a place—for the following August. It was not what I wanted, but at least it would put off the evil moment when I would have to leave the safety of institutional life and face the world outside.

It was thus in a state of some insecurity about my future employment, my personal development and my sexuality that I left school at the age of seventeen years one month. Despite my many criticisms of life at school I was very sad to leave and remember having a tear in my eye and a lump in my throat.

In the school's eyes I was well adjusted, popular and well equipped to face the future—I had succeeded. In my own eyes my self-confidence was at an all-time low, I was unsure of myself and felt singularly ill equipped to meet what lay in store for me—I had survived.

Chapter 4

Out of the Cocoon

My year at Pembridge Place did a great deal to restore my general confidence. First, I found myself being stretched academically for the first time in many years, for, contrary to my expectations, the shorthand typing course was hard work and required a great deal of concentration and effort on my part. The college had very high standards, demanding that all students made the grade even if it meant hours of evening work.

Also, unlike school, Pembridge did try to encourage independence in its inmates. The rooms were comfortable, and each resident was allocated a bed with interior sprung mattress, a large wardrobe and a chest of drawers. My room I shared with three other boys, one of whom had also just left Linden Lodge. Apart from set times for meals and classes, there were very few rules and those that remained were so stupid that they deserved to be broken. For example, although some of the students were well into their forties, everyone had to be in by 10.30 in the evening. Residents were allowed one late key a week, which enabled you to come in whatever time you liked. Three friends and I devised a scheme whereby we would each book one late key a week and then all go out together on each occasion, and thus gain four late keys. A certain degree of cooperation was needed from someone in the college, who would volunteer to adjust our IN/OUT markers and answer any awkward questions; but if I was ever wanted there was always someone to say that I was in the bath, in the toilet or in another room and they would pass the message on. The other way around the late key problem, if one was lucky enough to stay out all night, was to return about 7.00 in the morning when the night lock was taken off. If I was challenged I would reply that I had been for an early morning walk or to get a newspaper for someone.

The other silly rule imposed a ten shilling fine on any man caught going up the girls' stairway. My friends and I all agreed that if it wasn't worth ten bob, it wasn't worth going up in the first place!

One thing noticeable by its absence was any form of organised evening activity. And, like school, Pembridge did not even possess a television. I never obtained an adequate explanation from either school or college why a television set was not installed in either of their lounges. Whether it was because the authorities thought that the blind didn't "watch" T.V., or because they thought it would interfere with studies, I will never know. There was not even a decent record player, and at times the atmosphere in the lounge was more akin to that of a church or a library than a place of relaxation and enjoyment.

However, my evenings were soon filled as I found female company. My first two girlfriends were fellow students, both partially sighted and both attractive. They did a great deal to improve my self-confidence, and I was proud that the two most desirable girls in the college had agreed to go out with me. Most evenings I took one of them to the pictures, theatre, out for a drink, or simply for a walk in the park. Embarrassing incidents in places like restaurants and toilets still happened, but they upset me less, because the person I was with had experienced such embarrassments for herself on other occasions, so we were jointly embarrassed but able to laugh and turn the disasters that befell us into talking points. One time when I was out with a girl I hooked something with my white stick, but carried on walking. I lifted my stick into my hand just as an irate woman hopped up like Cinderella to claim her shoe! On another occasion we went to the pictures, and I found myself sitting on the floor under the seats. Vandals had been at work and, not content with ripping the seat, they had stolen it. And a third time, in a crowded restaurant, I handed my girlfriend a serviette as we sat down. She had neglected to tell me, however, that there were lighted candles on the table, and as I reached my hand across the flame I caught the end of the paper napkin and it flared up in my hand. The fire was eventually put out by the waiter with the contents of the water jug, but, needless to say, we never went back to that restaurant.

My next girlfriend at Pembridge, however, was sighted and a member of the domestic staff. It was a stated rule that students must not go out with members of staff, but, as I said before, rules are meant to be broken. Vicki was an extremely tall girl (over six feet) who helped in the kitchen and doubled up as the "egg and chips" cook on Monday evenings when the main cook had her night off. Whether it was my fatal charm that attracted her or my ability to consume more egg and chips than my colleagues, I do not know, but the fact that a sighted girl—who did not even need glasses!—had found me attractive did a great deal to boost my ego. Ironically, Vicki's interest in me, developed into more of "a passion", which I found a bit overwhelming, and at one point I wished that she had chosen someone else.

Towards the end of my year at Pembridge my social activities had to take second place to my studies. I had to work extremely hard to attain the standards required. Braille shorthand was not easy to master. I had, for example, to learn over 2,000 different braille signs and be able to recall them and write them at four characters per second in order to reach a speed of 120 w.p.m. Once having written a passage in braille, I then had to transcribe it on to a typewriter with the minimum of errors. Typing too was complicated. I had to learn how to do tabulations, invoices, legal documents and advertisements. Because I could not see what I was typing I had to develop the ability to concentrate on one thing and exclude all others. If I made a mistake I was not allowed to correct it, I had simply to rip the paper out and start all over again. As some of the tabulations took nearly two hours to complete, I was particularly careful not to make an error at the end. The powers of concentration learned then have helped me in later life and given me a degree of single-mindedness that I might not otherwise have had. I passed my 100 w.p.m. shorthand examination and my intermediate stage typing with distinction and was pleased with myself.

Unfortunately, the passing of exams also meant the passing of my school and college life, and once again I had to face the grim reality that very soon I would be a "worker". The thought of entering the outside world (that is how I still thought of it) worried me a great deal, but I decided to think positive and began to search for a job before one was found for me. One evening someone read out of an evening paper that a bureau in the West End was looking for shorthand typists. I rang the number in the ad and was asked to go for an interview. I dressed in my best suit and took my shorthand machine along ready for a test. I found the office near Oxford Street, quite easily, and was eventually shown into a large room crammed full with people sitting at desks. I was asked to take a seat by the desk of the lady I had spoken to on the telephone, and my interview began. She asked several questions about my educational qualifications and my shorthand. The bureau did not actually employ typists, it found jobs for them. I felt extremely stupid, but brightened up a little when she said that there should be no problem in finding me a job and that she would try first the Civil Service. I was not sure what that august body did but agreed that she should have a go. I kept very quiet about my blunder at college, but eventually was to laugh about it with the other students, especially when the bureau telephoned to say that they had arranged an interview and test for me at the Civil Service Shorthand and Typing School. I passed both tests with flying colours, and two weeks later received a letter offering me a job as a grade 1 typist at the Board of Trade in Victoria, at a starting salary of £12.50 a week. This appeared a great deal of money to me and I had no hesitation in accepting the post.

In the last weeks at Pembridge another "leaver's conference" was arranged and at this I astounded the gathering when I revealed that I had already found a job for myself. Some of those assembled, congratulated me on my initiative, but others, I think, resented the fact that I had done things without consulting them. Why they should have resented me saving them work I do not know.

Thus, I took the next big step in my life and started work on 16th August 1968 at the age of eighteen.

My feelings on the morning of my first day at work were, I suspect, similar to those of anyone in the same situation, blind or not. I felt a hollow in the pit of my stomach and the thought of food made me rush for the nearest lavatory. I donned my best suit and matching tie, and, after visiting the toilet about ten times, I was ready to go. I checked I had everything, gave my shoes a last polish, and then set off. Fortunately the route to work was very easy, involving only one bus virtually from door to door. My mother caught the same bus to get to her job, so we left together. Once aboard my mother talked almost incessantly in a valiant attempt to take my mind off what lay ahead, but after about fifteen minutes she had to get off and I was on my own. I had asked the conductor to put me off at the right stop but this did not prevent me from sitting there worrying: would he remember? I dreaded going past my stop and being late on my first morning. However, the conductor did not forget and helped me off the bus directly outside the Board of Trade offices.

It was quite easy to tap along the side of the building and find the main entrance, and with shaking hands, a pale face and a feeling in my stomach as though I had just disembarked from a cross-channel ferry after a bad crossing, I entered the office block. The doorman took me up to the office of the typing Controller, who, after taking down several particulars, led me in turn to the seventh floor of the building where my typing pool was situated. As the

Controller showed me the way, my stomach nearly fell through the floor—

I would never find my way around this labyrinth of corridors on my own.

We eventually arrived at the typing pool and I was introduced to Mrs. Freeman, who was to be my supervisor. As we talked I was aware that all work in the office had stopped, and I felt I knew not how many pairs of eyes looking at me. But Mrs. Freeman saw that I was very nervous and did what she could to put me at my ease. She introduced me to everyone in the office in turn, and my sense of gloom lifted somewhat when I found that I was sharing an office with fifteen women, some of whom sounded very nice indeed. None of them, I suspected, would be interested in football, but there would be other compensations.

My desk I soon learned was placed right at the front of the office, with the door directly behind me. Thus, I had to turn to face the whole office every time I wanted to go out. I would have preferred to sit somewhere in the corner where I could hide and slip in and out of the room unnoticed.

I was informed that my typewriter was still with the engineers having the braille scale fitted, so I just sat and tried to look interested in my studies of my shorthand manual. But my efforts to go unnoticed were doomed. A messenger came in and Mrs. Freeman asked him if he would show me where the toilets were. Very self-conscious, we set off arm in arm. He had no idea how to guide me, so eventually I asked him to walk in front and I would follow him. He showed me where the various facilities were, then made me blush profusely by insisting on coming into the toilet cubicle with me to make sure I knew exactly where the pan was! When the messenger and I returned to the typing pool, my face was still a bright shade of red. I hoped earnestly that I would be spared any further such attentions; the location was straightforward enough and I was sure I could find it easily on my own. But word had got around amongst the messengers, and every fifteen minutes or so one or other of them would sidle up to me and utter out of the side of his mouth but still loud enough for everyone else to hear,

"Do you want to go to the John mate?" or, "Are you O.K. for the Kasi?" My reaction to their solicitations was to blush yet again and refuse their offers, even though at one point I was absolutely bursting to go.

At about 10.30 I heard someone bang on the door and yell "tea". Mrs. Freeman came over and asked me for my cup, and when I replied that I didn't have one silence fell over the office. I felt as if I had committed a cardinal sin or uttered a blasphemy. Well, I suppose not having one's own cup in the Civil Service in those days was tantamount to sacrilege! When the office had got over the shock, someone volunteered to lend me a spare cup, and I was entreated to bring my own the next day. The tea was disgusting but I must have begun to relax as I was able to eat a couple of rolls without immediately bringing them up again. Two of the girls in the office offered to take me to lunch at 12.30 and show me the canteen. I looked forward to this with mixed pleasure and foreboding as I learned that the canteen was self-service.

Just before 12.30 the moment I had been dreading arrived. "To pee or not to pee?" I decided that I could hold on no longer and so with crossed fingers (and legs) I rose to my feet, picked up my towel and teacup and aimed myself at where I hoped the door was. I found it first time. Once through the door I scurried down the corridor. I was convinced that everyone in the office had been watching me and waiting for me to commit my first blunder.

Once in the loo I placed my cup on the window-sill and walked towards the urinal, but as I stepped up I found to my dismay that there was somebody already standing there. He did not take too kindly to being propelled into the urinal but soon calmed down when he realised that I could not see. It was somewhat shakily that I made my way back to the pool, my face even redder than before, and managed to locate my desk first time. I gratefully slumped in my chair determined to drink nothing more during the day, so as to avoid going to the toilet again until I got home. Just then Mrs. Freeman said that it was time for lunch and asked if I wanted one of the porters to take me to the toilet. When I replied that I had already been, she was astonished and gasped "What, on your own?"

Unfortunately, my cockney cheek asserted itself at that moment and before I could stop myself I blurted out that I had been going to the toilet on my own for about seventeen years. I could have bitten my tongue once I had spoken, but luckily Mrs. Freeman did not take offence and from that moment on she treated me like anyone else in the office. If I was late or my work was bad I got told off. If my work was good she would give me credit as it was due. If I needed to leave early for something special she would allow me to do so.

Lunch with the two girls passed without any mishaps and this pleasant lunch date was to be repeated over the rest of the week. The girls were friendly and talkative, and making friends with them allayed many of my fears and eased the tension for me.

In the afternoon of my first day I had my first shorthand call. Mrs. Freeman asked one of the girls to take me to the appropriate office, and I managed to acquit myself satisfactorily.

So the first week passed smoothly until the Friday, when I was again having lunch with the two girls from the office. As we sat eating we were spotted by one of the waitresses, who announced in front of the two girls and half the restaurant that I was supposed to sit in the main canteen as there was a table "reserved for the blind" by the exit door. I could have throttled her, and I vowed that as often as possible I would break the rules and sit where the "normal" sat. I did, however, swallow my pride when lunching on my own, because the special table had the luxury of waitress service. The swallowing of my pride I had to balance against many possible embarrassments, such as taking someone else's dinner or spilling custard down somebody's back (both of which I did in fact manage to do at one time or another). The self-service area was massive and there was a long walk between the food hotplates and the cash desk and cutlery table. Then, finding an empty table among a hundred or more was all but impossible for me. I therefore admitted defeat as gracefully as I could, but resented the special table the whole time I was in the Civil Service. When someone voiced the assumption that "of course being blind I would like to sit with other blind people", I asked where the tables were for blacks, the one-legged or lovers of cats. The prominent position of the table, immediately by the exit door, did not help since I was already slightly paranoid and thought everyone was watching me. The other occupants of the table were also not inspiring company, so I used to eat my lunch as quickly as possible and then go for a walk or sit in the office and read.

Life at work soon settled down into a boring routine, but I had one piece of luck, the by-product of yet another disaster. I seem throughout my life to have been followed by misfortune in toilets. On this occasion I was paying one of my daily visits when, on putting my towel on the window ledge, I heard a crash and the sound of breaking crockery. I had carelessly failed to check to see if anything was on the ledge, and had managed to knock over someone's hallowed cup and saucer. The owner of the receptacle said that it did not matter and we began talking about how I was finding the work. Peter seemed a nice bloke, and whenever we encountered one another we had a chat. When I mentioned one day how bored I was at lunch times he offered to show me the local market. This offer I readily accepted and Peter and I went to lunch together nearly every day from then on. Those excursions at lunch times with Peter broke the monotony of the days which, only a few weeks after starting work, I already found tedious and unstimulating.

The work, when I had it, I enjoyed, but all too often there was no work to do. I was one of four shorthand typists in the office, and we would serve between us some twelve officers. The system was that the officer would telephone when he wanted a shorthand typist, then one of us would go, take the dictation and return to the pool to transcribe it. When all the officers were busy we had more shorthand calls than we could handle: when they weren't busy we had more typists than work. The other three could see and therefore did copy-typing to fill in the time. I could not do this, and so simply had to sit and read or go to sleep. When work was at its worst I would count myself lucky if I had one day's work in a whole week.

Many of the officers began to ask for me personally, which pleased me, though not all my colleagues. If I was busy the officer would usually choose to wait until I was free. I am not sure whether they found my work good, or just enjoyed my tendency to chat, but no matter what the reason I was grateful to them for their vote of confidence.

At first I took a book to read in the slack periods, but later added a wireless and earphone and then my talking book machine to my equipment. In the summer I would listen to the test match commentaries, and some of the officers acquired the habit of ringing me just to get the latest test score. I listened to the radio so much that I became a walking Radio Times and an authority on every programme from "Waggoner's Walk" to "Woman's Hour".

Anybody who thinks he would like to do nothing all day has surely never experienced the boredom that such a life of leisure brings with it.

My social life, now I was living at home again, was none too active either. Apart from my friends Alan and Keith, I had nobody my age to talk to or even to go out for a drink with. Most evenings I spent watching television, listening to records or occasionally going out with my mother. Things however livened up at the weekends when I began to make pilgrimages to Birmingham. Towards the end of my time at Pembridge I had made friends with a boy from Birmingham, named John, and he had come home with me at weekends. Then John decided to have a party at the end of term to celebrate leaving college and his twenty-first birthday. Several of the students from Pembridge travelled up, and I went with my mum and future step-father. At the party I met John's sister Joan, who was both sighted and attractive. We liked each other from the outset and began going out together. Thus, every Friday at five o'clock I would rush from the office to Victoria Coach Station to board the coach for Birmingham. At the other end I was met and usually whisked off to some pub or another.

One of these pubs had live music, and one Friday night I was coaxed into getting up and singing with the folk band. I was an immediate success and became almost a part-time member of the group, singing Friday and Saturday nights and sometimes lunchtime on Sunday. The drink usually flowed fast and furious and by Sunday night I was well and truly waterlogged and used to look forward to the quiet week in which to recover before the following Friday. My weekends thus made up for the week.

If I had not had that outlet I am not sure that I could have coped with the depression of work: I lived in fear that something would happen to stop me going. Yet it was my own conscious decision that brought things to an end. After I had made the journey weekly for some nine months, I realised that both Joan and her parents were building up hopes for the future which involved me and marriage. I had been colluding with these plans, and had actually suggested (without prompting) that Joan and I should get engaged. Yet once I had committed myself, I discovered that while I liked Joan a great deal, I did not love her. For both our sakes I had to act quickly. So I told Joan that I did not feel there was any point in carrying on as I had had second thoughts about marriage and our future together.

It would be better that we did not see each other again.

That decision, and the execution of it, was probably one of the hardest things I have had to do in my life. Not only had I to hurt someone I liked a great deal, but I also had to cut myself off from the fun at the pub, the singing and good fellowship—the very things that were keeping me sane. I realised that I had fallen into a trap which I suspect many blind people fall into: like with Vicki before her, I had been flattered that Joan, sighted and herself attractive, found me attractive. Because I found it so difficult to meet girls in the first place, let alone one who could cope with the embarrassment of a blind boyfriend, I had allowed the relationship to develop a long way, for fear almost of not finding another girl. Yet I realised now that Joan and I had very little in common: for several weeks before the end we had had nothing other than trivia to talk about with each other.

Yet my weekends in Birmingham did not end after all. Another friend, Graham, offered me a bed at weekends, and I continued to sing with the group on Fridays and Saturdays.

Meanwhile, changes were taking place in my family life. My brother John had married some months earlier and was, by the time of my split up with Joan, the proud father of a baby girl. I was an uncle and my mum was a grandmother for the first time. My mother had obtained her divorce from my father, and she and I were now living alone. But it happened that my sister-in-law's father had just become a widower, and since he was frequently at my brother's house visiting his granddaughter just as my mum was, they became friends. Eventually they decided to get married—which made all the family happy though at the same time it created utter confusion as to who was related to whom. With my mother marrying my sister-in-law's father, my brother became married to his step-sister thus making his own daughter his step-niece. My step-sister and sister-in-law became one and the same. It was all very confusing but I think I have just about worked it out now.

My step-father had another daughter and a son and they both came to live with us in our large Victorian House. When my second step-sister got married, however, my parents decided that the house was too big and too old and decided to buy a smaller one in Enfield. About three months after Joan and I had broken up, we moved. This meant that I had to learn the geography of my new area and master another route to work, which involved a train and two tube journeys. As I was now quite a way out of London I did not see very much of my friends Alan and Keith, and my weekends in Birmingham too finally ended. The depression I suffered during the week now spilled over into the weekends again, and my self-esteem and self-confidence ebbed rapidly.

However, it has been said that "as one door closes another one opens, and my door opened when I received a telephone call from the teacher who had first introduced me to folk music. She asked whether I would be interested in singing in a folk group with her and two others. I jumped at the chance, not only to sing again, but also to meet new people. The enjoyment I got from involvement in the group replaced that which I had got singing at the weekends in Birmingham, and went some way towards offsetting the boredom I was suffering at work. The group was also the means through which, later, I was to meet my wife.

Chapter 5

New Beginnings

By late 1969 the folk group had begun to make a name for itself and we were asked to play at several venues. I became great friends with the other male singer, another Mike, and we would often meet after work for a drink or stay at each other's houses and practice a new song or arrangement. We enjoyed each other's company and had a similar sense of humour. Then one of the two girl singers, Josephine, invited Mike and me to her office Xmas party. We had both met friends of Josephine's that we fancied and half hoped that we might be able to reacquaint ourselves with the girls in question. Unfortunately, when we arrived both girls were already attached, and, there being no other available females, Mike and I decided that we would have a good attempt at getting thoroughly drunk.

I am ashamed to say that we both succeeded only too well and by closing time we could barely stand, let alone walk. Mike, being sighted, was better off than me in that he went through three stages of inebriation i.e. drunk, blind drunk and paralytic drunk. I, of course, missed out the first and started at blind drunk. But we apparently fooled the others at the party (or they were as drunk as we) because we were invited by the assembled throng to go and have something to eat with them. The mere mention of food made me feel ill but I was past caring and would have been game for anything, the more so because the boy with Maureen, the girl I fancied, decided not to eat, but to go home. Maureen bade him goodnight and took my arm to lead the way. Her escort called her back to say goodnight properly and I, not wishing to witness any scenes of passion, and since I was dying to go to the toilet anyway, wandered with Mike down a nearby lane and proceeded to moisten the plaster of someone's wall. It was then that I noticed that I had, on my shoulder, Maureen's handbag. Mike and I must have looked an interesting couple emerging from an alleyway adjusting our dress, with me gaily swinging a black handbag and whistling. Maureen came up to me and again took my arm. She explained that she had met the boy only that evening and had been trying to get away from him all night. Maureen managed to steer me very well. It is not easy to guide a blind person at the best of times, but with a drunk blind person, it is nigh on impossible.

At the restaurant I slumped into a vacant chair and tried desperately to make intelligible conversation. All the time I was speaking, however, I felt a rising urge to be sick and when the food finally arrived the smell of the greasy hamburgers and chips was too much for me. I told Mike that he was going to take me to the toilet and we only just made it in time. After my stomach had emptied its contents, I tried to regain my composure and we returned to the table. I felt acutely aware of the startling impression I must have been making—blind drunk and sick—but Maureen seemed oblivious to it all and when we finished the meal she offered to see me home! Yes, right first time, SHE saw ME home! I had obviously no chance of getting a train to Enfield at one in the morning, so as my brother lived not far from Maureen, I decided to give him a ring and ask whether I could come and stay the night. We said goodnight to everyone and Maureen found a phone box that was working. Still somewhat unsure of my co-ordination, I dialled my brother's number and got him out of bed. He agreed that I could come and gave Maureen directions on where he lived. Then, after I replaced the receiver, we began talking and two hours later, still talking, we left the phone box happy and in love.

The Dutch courage within me had done wonders and I had even asked Maureen if she would see me again. She had said yes, and written her telephone number on an old envelope. We managed to hail a taxi and arrived at my brother's flat at about 3 a.m. He answered the door in his underpants (not a pretty sight whether you are drunk or sober). We had asked the taxi man to wait, and him seeing Maureen's predicament i.e. her having to cope with a drunken blind man, he had agreed. Maureen and I parted with me promising to ring her the next day.

Maureen seeing me home did not seem as embarrassing as I had thought. She seemed to take everything in her stride: and as she seemed not to mind, I didn't either.

The next morning, when I awoke, I thought I was dead. My stomach felt as though it had no bottom to it. My eyes and head ached terribly and when the smell of breakfast reached my nostrils I rushed headlong for the bathroom. My tongue felt as though it was too big for my mouth and I had a thirst like never before. I couldn't face any food and my brother put a very fragile creature on a bus heading towards Victoria. When I arrived at work I slumped into my seat and half sat, half lay over my typewriter, groaning and praying that nobody would ask me to do any shorthand for them. Various colleagues asked me about the night before, but I was in no mood for lively conversation. At lunch time I managed to consume a glass of milk, which made me feel slightly better. By about 3.00 I apparently looked half human again and was able to tell the girls in the office about my drunken night out. All were eager to know when I was going to phone Maureen. I replied that I didn't know if I would. Supposing she had given me her number just to get out of the phone box? Come to think of it, supposing she hadn't given me her number at all but had merely written "Mickey Mouse" and given me the number for London Zoo? I extracted the crumpled envelope from my pocket and, half in dread, handed it to one of the girls to see what was written there. It was a work telephone number indeed, and the girl did nothing but go straight up to the phone and dial it. When it was answered at the other end she thrust the receiver into my hands. I was terrified. What would she sound like, would she have forgiven me for my previous night's conduct? But when Maureen spoke she sounded almost as if she had been waiting for my call, and when after a few minutes I suggested she come over to my house that night (Christmas Eve) for a party, she agreed. From 'then on we saw each other regularly and in April 1971 we became engaged.

With Maureen shortly after meeting 1969

Mike and Maureen on their Wedding Day 1 July 1972

Whilst my social life flourished my daily routine at work became ever more tedious. As a means of earning extra money, and giving myself something to do, I made contact with someone in a clothing warehouse and spent a large part of the day selling ladies' clothing around the office building. During a good week I could sell as much as £250 worth of stuff, for which I received about £30, so at times was earning twice as much from my tally round as I did from being a shorthand typist. I also ran the office sweepstake, and a weekly football pontoon involving over 80 people. At Christmas time, or when someone was leaving, it was invariably me who would arrange the party. Yet despite all this activity my work continued to depress me thoroughly, and I decided that action was required.

What could I do however? I had three 'O' levels and qualifications in shorthand typing. I clearly needed further qualifications, so I decided to start enrolling in a correspondence course for 'A' level English. My essays I could type at work and most of the lessons I had arranged to receive on tape. My former English teacher, with whom I had kept in touch, said that she would give me some private tuition on the Shakespeare and Chaucer. Maureen also helped, by reading things through to me, and I enjoyed the studying and the stimulation it gave me. I took the examination as an external candidate from the school I had attended and surprised everyone, including myself, by passing it with a good grade. I was not as stupid as I looked, and, more importantly, I now knew it.

One occupation open to the blind that appealed to me was computer programming, for which I could get training in the Civil Service, so I decided next to improve my basic level of maths. My arithmetic ability was generally good but I had done very little algebra or geometry. Again, I managed to find one of the teachers at the school who would help, so I visited the school for a class once a week, and by the time applications for a computer programming course were due I had at least covered the basics. I attended an aptitude test and passed that, then waited for the Civil Service circular. When the vacancy list did finally appear I was bitterly disappointed. The nearest vacancies were in Newport or Norwich, and would obviously involve my leaving London and my family. What was more, this was the year, 1972, in which Maureen and I were planning to get married. On the one hand, I felt even more acutely the need to find another job which paid better, as it hurt my male pride to have a wife who earned considerably more than I did. On the other hand, I would have enough to do with the wedding and adjusting to married life, without the added worry of a new job, travelling and an unknown environment. I decided not to apply for the programming course on that occasion and to wait for the next one.

Marriage required many adjustments by both Maureen and myself. I have said earlier that one never ceases to make adjustments, as every new situation brings with it fresh difficulties and problems, and one of the biggest adjustments in marriage for both of us was to the necessary reversals of roles. Maureen had to be the dominant partner in many practical situations where traditionally the male would be the one to assert himself. For instance, I could not drive a car. When ordering food in restaurants she invariably would have to assume command. And decorating a home was extremely difficult for me. Even the selection of furniture and furnishings for our new home I had to leave almost entirely to her, as I could not see colours.

By nature Maureen is a shy, retiring person who likes to be unnoticed in a crowd, and to be forced, as she often was, into situations where she had to be forceful and assertive placed a heavy burden on her. I, in contrast, am quite assertive and at times forceful, but had often to be content with playing a secondary part, which I also found difficult. Some of these problems, I think, were recognised in the apparently insensitive remarks passed by some of our friends prior to the wedding. Frequently people told Maureen that she was marvellous for "taking on such a responsibility". Others asked her whether she was at all worried about marrying a blind man. Things got so bad at one time that she had to ask me whether there was anything that I hadn't told her about myself. She was worried that she was not worried, she said, and thought she might be overlooking some aspect of our future which she would not be able to cope with.

What I was most apprehensive about was how Maureen's parents would take to having a blind son-in-law. All parents want the "best" for their children and, marrying someone with a disability can all too readily be classed as "second best". But in the event Maureen's parents could not have been warmer or more responsive to me. They must have had their doubts and worries, but they never showed them to either Maureen or myself.

In the event, then, the wedding went off happily, and Maureen and I settled down in our new home.

For me, marriage brought with it one invaluable luxury. For the first time since I had been blind, I had someone with whom I could be totally myself and share my moments of frustration, joy or disappointment. Virtually from the moment of the accident that blinded me, I had felt almost obliged to put a brave face on things. Whenever I had been sad or depressed I had been told to cheer up. Whenever I had felt particularly lacking in self-confidence and my morale was low, I had been told to "smile, it may never happen". I had begun to be afraid of showing any of my emotions in case they upset other people, for I had become aware that when someone with a disability becomes anxious or upset, that anxiety is only too easily passed on to the non-disabled helper or relation, who then feels twice as bad for not being able to relieve the cause of the upset. This fear of creating anxiety in others is very often the reason why the disabled person hides his feelings and tries to "soldier on" regardless. People so often assume that disabled people "seem to be happy" despite their problems; but I suspect that in many cases an apparently carefree attitude really reflects a feeling that they need to put on a "good show". For newly disabled people this "putting on a show" can be extremely dangerous, because it may deny them the opportunity to truly mourn the loss of whatever function they no longer have. Of course at times I missed being able to see, and of course at times the frustrations my blindness caused me made me resentful and angry. With Maureen I had at last someone with whom I could express these things, and that, for me, was an important, and unexpected bonus of being married.

After my marriage, the most important event in 1972 was my return to active sport. Since leaving school, my sporting activities had been very much confined to those of a spectator, since there appeared to be no sports facilities locally that would accept a blind person as an ordinary member. So I was delighted when an old school friend asked me if I would like to play cricket for a blind sports club based in London. I jumped at the chance and began to play matches for the club in Regents Park.

Our team, however, was very mixed, both in ability and interest in the game. I and two or three of my friends wanted to improve the standard of play; while others, mainly the older blind people, many of whom had never had the mobility training and opportunities that I and my friends had had, treated it as an afternoon outing which required very little commitment and even less effort. The younger element in the club were however the minority, and we soon felt that our opinions and wishes were being paid very little attention. I tried to get elected on to the committee but failed: most of the other members felt that at twenty-two I was too young. As the year progressed it became more and more apparent that we and the more established members of the club would never see eye to eye, so rather than stay and possibly create discontent in the club it seemed best for those of us with serious sporting ambition to leave, and form our own sports club which could do the things that we wanted.

In early January 1973 a group of eight met to try to work out aims for our new club. We wanted to make sport available to, and draw our members from, the whole of the metropolitan area of London, so we decided to call ourselves the Metropolitan Sports and Social Club for the Visually Handicapped (which name has thankfully been shortened to METRO). We drew up a constitution and set of rules, and elected a committee of five of which I was to be Chairman. Our basic aims were simple but specific. We wanted:

71

(a) to provide the visually handicapped with as wide a range of sporting activities (both competitive and non-competitive) as possible;

(b) to provide a variety of social activities and interests for members;

(c) to provide the means—through sporting and social events—of meeting and mixing with able-bodied people, so as to improve generally the sighted person's understanding of the needs of the V.H., and assist their integration into the community;

(d) to provide, where possible, financial help so as to ensure that the criteria for participation is the strength of need or enjoyment on the part of the player, rather than the strength of his or her pocket.

We decided that initially we should concentrate on the sports of which we personally had had experience, and so for the first nine months we focused on cricket and football. Both sports are very popular amongst blind and partially sighted sportsmen and, with slight adaptations to the rules, can be very enjoyable, demanding quite a high degree of skill and alertness from the participants. It has remained our principle, with all the sports, to use as few mechanical or electronic aids as possible, so that the games are reasonably easy to learn, and cost as little as possible for basic equipment.

Cricket, for instance, we keep as close to the ordinary game as possible. We play with four totally blind and seven partially sighted players on each side. For a ball we use a small football — which has had the valve removed and thirty or forty pieces of lead shot or ball bearings inserted in it. The pieces of lead rattle inside the ball when it is on the ground or in the air. The playing rules vary according to the category of sight of the players; that is, when a totally blind batsman is batting, the ball must bounce twice before the batting crease, thus enabling the batsman to locate the ball on the first bounce and, having estimated its speed and height, play a shot at the second bounce. All totally blind batsmen have a runner to complete their runs and are allowed two leg-before-wicket decisions before being declared out; and they cannot be stumped. And when the totally blind player is fielding he is allowed to catch the ball after it has bounced once. This is quite difficult to achieve as the ball, if hit with the full face of the bat, travels extremely quickly. Most totally blind players when bowling ask the batsman if he is ready, and then bowl the ball according to the direction of his voice. If the batsman tries to cheat by standing wide of the stumps, the blind bowler asks his direction from the wicket keeper instead.

For the partially sighted players, the rules are almost exactly the same as for sighted players in ordinary cricket. The main exception is that the ball must pitch once before the batting crease, to enable him time at least to glimpse it before it shatters his wicket.

The stumps themselves can be ordinary full size ones, though many clubs use slightly larger and wider stumps to give the bowler a fairer chance. The actual pitch length for visually handicapped cricket is reduced from 22 yards to 18, as it is extremely difficult to bowl a large ball fast over a long distance. There are several visually handicapped sides playing cricket, and virtually all play matches against fully sighted opposition. Although it looks easy it is an extremely difficult and skilful game to play, and I remember that one sighted side from a Round Table in Romford recorded a score of only 16 against my club, which was the lowest score we had ever been faced with.

The following year we offered to play them in daylight and it made no difference!

Unforeseen problems can, of course, arise. For instance, a blind fielder may be fielding too close to the bat when an equally blind batsman plays a shot, and the fielder ends up with a mouth full of willow. And when our club decided that we should try to look the part of cricketers and invest in cricket whites, one or two of the partially sighted bowlers found it almost impossible to distinguish between fielders, batsmen and wicket keeper. We decided therefore that each team should have their own coloured kit and thus provide maximum contrast to the colour of the ball and stumps. But all in all we have found our matches demanding, competitive and exhilarating.

Football also needs adaptation according to different sight categories. Matches for the partially sighted may be either eleven-a-side or five-a-side, but they are mostly the latter. The ball must not go above head height, to help the partially sighted player keep it within his field of vision. Some partially sighted players, however, may not be able to see where their own players are situated for passing, and have to rely on their team-mates to call for the ball or indicate in some other way where they are. The equipment and the rest of the rules are the same as for sighted players, except that a contrasting coloured ball may be used on particularly difficult surfaces: for instance, we avoid playing with a white ball on a beige or white floor, or with a brown ball on a dark wooden floor. Some clubs have experimented with spotted footballs to provide the maximum degree of contrast. Similarly, the colour of the partially sighted player's team shirt or opposition strip can be of crucial importance, and a great deal more time than usual goes into choosing clothing to try to suit all the team's sight problems.

Football for the totally blind has more differences from ordinary football. Eleven-a-side football is virtually never played when all players are totally blind—we play five-a-side or mixed five-a-side. The football is doctored in the same way as for cricket, with shot or ball bearings placed inside it so that the blind players can hear the ball. It takes a great deal of practice, but we learn to run with the ball, pass it, head it and shoot it at the goal. The five-a-side matches where all the players are totally blind are played either indoors or on outside pitches where all obstacles have been carefully removed. When playing outside, we use an area roughly similar in size to a tennis court, measuring from 30 to 60 metres long by 15 to 25 metres wide. High netting, walls or some form of fencing placed around the whole of the perimeter prevents the ball from constantly going out of play. The goals are usually large wooden boards measuring about seven feet by five feet, attached to the fencing in the middle of each end of the pitch. Care is obviously taken to ensure that the goals do not protrude and create a danger to the unseeing player.

The footballer's own orientation tells him where he is on the playing field in relation to his own, and his opponents goal; but if for any reason he becomes disorientated, he can either call his own goal keeper and use his reply as a location point, or go to the side netting and judge his position from there. He can usually hear his opponents running up with the ball or coming in for a tackle. Most players try to kick the ball and not the opposition, and the referee usually has to display considerable discretion as to what constitutes a foul and what an accident. The game is fiercely competitive and, despite obvious dangers, very few injuries occur.

The main surprise for anyone just happening to arrive at a match involving totally blind sides would not be in the players but in the spectators. Because all the players are using their hearing to the utmost, the crowd are always asked, whilst the ball is in play, to keep perfectly silent, so there is none of the shouting, chanting or commenting usual at a football match— except, of course, when a goal is scored. The games are usually very good to watch, and I continue to find "blind" football one of the most exciting and demanding sports to play.

Our main problem with blind football has been in forming the teams. The total number of active, able, young blind sportsmen is very small, and to find ten living in any one area, even the size of

London, is unlikely. Consequently, a mixed five-a-side game has evolved, with two partially sighted and three totally blind players on each side. Only the totally blind players can score and the partially sighted players are given the positions of goal keeper and ball distributor. The game is played exactly the same as ordinary five-a-side football, with a great deal of team work required between the partially sighted players on the field and the three strikers. This game possibly demands even more skill and speed on the part of the totally blind forwards than blind five-a-side, because they are likely to be tackled by the partially sighted player and have a partially sighted rather than a totally blind goal keeper to put the ball past.

Both of these last sports demand great personal skill and considerable ability to play as a team member. As well as being able to control a football when running with it at your feet, you have also to be able to hear where the opposing and your own team members are, to recognise your team members when they call for a pass, and then to pass the ball accurately. Both sports we performed on ordinary sports fields—we played football at Holland Park School as part of an evening class and cricket at Regent's Park, where we booked a pitch like any other cricket club. But we provoked on occasion some very strange responses.

I remember in particular one football night at the school when, it being a dry night, we decided to play outside on the tarmac area, and mystified the students in the other classes who were staring out of their classroom windows, wondering no doubt how on earth we were managing to play in pitch darkness!

Similarly, when we played cricket in the park, at sight of a group of grown men playing with a large football, quite a large crowd might gather to watch the loonies at play. Or others would think that we were just mucking around, and proceed to stroll right across the playing area or kick the ball in an effort to be helpful. My most vivid memory of such public ineptitude is of one attractive young lady who in the midst of a match deposited herself near the middle of the pitch and proceeded to apply her sun tan lotion. She must have altered her ideas suddenly when the ball hit her on the head and eleven men came rushing towards her with their arms out in front, all groping apparently for her face.

The club soon became popular and the membership grew very quickly. And as more members joined, requests came for sports not hitherto covered, such as swimming and athletics. Both athletics and swimming I had been involved with at school, and felt that the blind could attain a high standard if enough effort were put into taking them seriously.

Athletics is now possibly the most rapidly developing sport for the blind and partially sighted in this country, if not the world. Many of the athletic events being performed by visually handicapped athletes would have been thought either impossible, or too dangerous, thirty years ago and so were not developed or studied, and even in the school I attended there was no real athletics attempted until my last year, when it was decided that perhaps our sports day should be run at the local athletic stadium instead of on the lawn at school. As more thought has been given to specific events over the years the standard and skill in the events has risen.

Adaptations to the events themselves have been remarkably few. In the throwing events, for example, the whole circle or run-up area can be used, so it is up to the thrower—whether partially sighted or totally blind—to devise his own particular method of running up straight and throwing in the correct direction. But the closer a blind athlete is able to get to the correct technique (a spin in the discus or run-up in the javelin) the further, potentially, he should be able to throw. The main event so far excluded, I think for obvious reasons, is hammer throwing, and having known many sighted throwers come perilously near to "hammering" the crowd, I do not regret it.

In the jumping events, pole vaulting is the only one to be thought either too dangerous or impracticable. In high jumping, both totally blind and partially sighted athletes can choose to use any of the usual methods of jumping, that is, western roll, scissors or Fosbury flop. For all jumps, however, perfection of technique and precision of run-up and take-off is important. Many totally blind jumpers do a standing jump and can clear heights up to 1 metre 35 or 1 metre 50. One jumper from my club who is totally blind has attempted, with some success, to perfect his Fosbury flop technique. I must say that this individual has more guts than I have, and many times I have stood beside the high jump envying his ability to run up to a bar he cannot see, jump into a space which he hopes is right and land on his back on mats he hopes are there. My one attempt at high jump since I have been blind ended in disaster when I ran at the bar, leapt into the air and landed on the same side as I had taken off! Everyone laughed except me.

Long and triple jump are also done by both partially sighted and totally blind. The totally blind jumper works out the paces in his run-up, sometimes even down to the last centimetre. In the long jump, some clubs and countries still feel that the athletes— totally blind or not—should have their jumps measured from the take-off board only, like "normal" athletes. Others feel that it is better to use a take-off area marked with plasticine or sand, and measure the jump from the jumper's front foot wherever it lands.

It is in running for the totally blind that perhaps the biggest differences with ordinary athletics are to be observed. Partially sighted runners are expected to run in lanes like ordinary athletes, and can therefore compete together. If possible, there is a free lane between each competitor to allow for a weaker sighted athlete straying from his lane without impeding the other runners. Totally blind runners, on the other hand, run individually against the clock. Several calling systems have been tried and tested, with varying success. The one favoured by most in my club is the number system, whereby each track lane is given a number. If the track, for example, has nine lanes the lanes will be numbered from one to nine, starting on the inside of the track. The runner's block will then be placed in the centre of lane five at the start. A caller is stationed either half way down the track for the 100 metres, or at the end of the 60 metres run, and will keep calling out the number of the lane the runner is in. So if he keeps dead straight only the number five will be called; if he deviates to the left he will hear the numbers go down from four to one; and if he goes to the right he will hear the numbers go up from six to nine. He will then know which way, and how much, to correct his line of running. Where longer distances are involved, the runner is allowed to run with someone, but his guide must be behind or level with him at all times, never in front. He can also, if he wishes, be attached in some way to the guide by means of a cord or elasticated rope.

The disadvantage with timed individual running is obvious: the blind athlete never has anyone to run against, and therefore may be denied just that extra incentive to improve his time. Experiments are under way to develop an electronic aid which can be operated by the "caller" at the end of the track. This device will emit a different note for left and right, and by this means each individual runner could be separately controlled so that it should eventually be possible for five or even six totally blind runners to run together, with individual "controllers" keeping them on the straight and narrow. This development should also mean that those athletes who become skilled enough at using these devices to run consistently, should be enabled to compete against sighted runners.

Since athletics offers each competitor the opportunity of achieving his or her own personal goal, whether it be 5 metres with the shot-put or 15 metres, it can provide the visually handicapped individual with a sense of achievement that may well be lacking in other aspects of his life.

Our club also managed to gain facilities at a swimming pool in a large London school and was thus able to offer supervision and tuition in swimming at times when we could have the pool to ourselves. This privacy is more important than one may think if one has never been a blind swimmer, torpedoing some unsuspecting member of the public or pushing them accidentally under the water. I have had some bad moments myself in public pools. I remember splashing about in a swimming bath with two blind friends when one of them, Carol, decided to get her own back after a ducking. Hearing me behind her she seized a leg, which she proceeded to pull and push in an effort to get its owner off balance. She yelled loudly "I've got him, I've got him". She had indeed "got him". Unfortunately, instead of me, it was an elderly gentleman out for an evening swim with his family.

Direction is not so much a problem to the swimmer as to the athlete. In competitions all the lanes are divided by ropes with cork floats on them so the blind swimmer can feel the lane ropes and adjust direction. At the ends of the pool there are usually officials to warn him that he is approaching the edge of the bath; and sometimes a thin piece of rope is placed in the water about a metre from the end, to indicate to him that it is time to turn or slow down.

All the usual swimming strokes are included in our swimming events, including butterfly and individual medleys, and some of the performances achieved by blind swimmers are as good as those of their sighted counterparts. Diving on the other hand is something which comparatively few blind people take up, because many eye complaints are irritated by the impact of the water or the pressure on the eyes when diving deep. In addition, of course, if you cannot see you cannot tell how deep the water is to judge the angle of your dive.

Swimming has the advantage that public swimming baths are numerous both in cities and in rural areas, and most people can reach a beach in some part of the country. Swimming I also see as important because it can give one the confidence to take up other water sports such as sailing, canoeing or water skiing.

With the addition of these two extra sports the administration of the club became more time consuming, and for a while, I was only too glad that I had all the time in the world to do it at work. I was always organising events, writing articles for magazines and compiling press releases. By the end of 1973 the club, which had started the year with 30 members, had raised over £500 and become a registered charity. It was also already being consulted by other bodies involved in developing sport for the disabled.

By the end of the year, too, I realised that I needed to think seriously again about changing my job. Three basic options appeared to be open to me: I could wait until the next computer programming course arose and apply for it, wherever the vacancy was; I could press to become a secretary within the Board of Trade; or I could try something quite different. The something I had in mind was to apply for training as a social worker.

All three options were fraught with difficulties. In favour of computer programming, I had passed my aptitude test and would almost certainly be offered training. But most of the vacancies were outside London, and Maureen and I had bought a house in Hornchurch, where we were very happy. Would it be fair to ask my wife to give that up and move to somewhere where neither of us might be happy? We both had strong family ties, and did not like the thought of being parted from them. Also, my sporting activities were almost as important to me as my employment. Could I give all that up now, having got it started? Pressing for a secretarial job, then, seemed to make better sense. Since joining the Civil Service I had managed to keep up my shorthand speeds and had passed several speed tests to earn a bonus each week. I had also passed my typing examinations, and thus with 130 w.p.m. shorthand and 65 w.p.m. typing, I was one of the best qualified shorthand typists in the department. I decided therefore, to push to become a personal secretary, the first blind or partially sighted secretary in the department, and actually managed to find a high- ranking official who would be willing to have me. But I encountered resistance on the management side. What would happen if my boss left and they couldn't find someone else to take me? How would I cope with certain parts of the work? If I really wanted to, I could probably get enough support from the union and the personnel department to obtain the post. But was it what I wanted? This brought me to my third option. For a long time, I had been drawn to thoughts of becoming a social worker. I had begun to study for another 'A' level, this time in Sociology, and I had applied to various Boroughs asking whether they would consider employing me. Only one of the Boroughs had given me an interview, and even this one made me no offer. There seemed to be a Catch 22 in operation: the local authorities would not employ me because I was not qualified, and the colleges would not accept me because I had no local authority experience.

I had in fact received the offer of a job in Blind Welfare, but I did not want to work with the blind, especially as a large part of my leisure time was taken up with blind people already. I did not want to isolate myself within the very narrow world of the visually handicapped. Although most people tried to put me off, I was determined to try to gain a place on a social work course and become a generic social worker handling the whole range of social problems, including child care and mental health. So I contacted the Social Workers' Advisory Service, who gave me the names and addresses of two colleges to apply to. The basic qualifications, luckily, were three 'O' levels and one 'A' level—exactly what I had. I applied and kept my fingers crossed, convinced that once I got an interview I would stand a chance.

A few weeks later I received an application form, which asked for a short 500-word statement about "why I wanted to become a social worker". After giving this a great deal of thought I decided to adopt the line that, having been a client of social workers for a number of years, I didn't think I could do much worse. This, though it had the merit of being true, was a calculated gamble. In order to make an impression I felt I had to write something different from "I want to help people and to be useful to society". I thus wrote about my experience on the receiving end and prayed it would not be received as "the angry client hits back". In January a circular came round in the Civil Service asking for applications for a computer course with the prospect of a job at Guildford; and in the same month there appeared to be some prospect at last of a personal secretary's position. Then, just as I had virtually given up hope, there arrived a request to attend for an interview for the social work course. I was in the very curious position of having three prospects to choose from!

So, of course, I sent in my application for the computer course and at the same time confirmed that I would be at the interview for the college.

When I arrived for that interview I felt a bit like I had on my first day at work: my stomach felt empty, and I realised how very important it was to me to pass the interview and to gain a place on the course. The first part of the assessment was an individual interview with one of the tutors. We talked at length about practical problems in the job, the academic demands that would be made on me and the emotional pressures involved. Then later in the day I took part in a group interview with five other candidates. This was apparently to see how I responded in groups, whether I could listen as well as contribute to a discussion, and so on. I left the college feeling mentally exhausted, but at the same time reasonably satisfied that I had done the best I could and that the rest was up to them. I had to trust them to judge me on my performance and not on their own feelings about whether or not a blind social worker could cope. The college apparently did exactly that, and two weeks after the interview I was offered a place on the course to commence the following September.

Maureen and I discussed together whether I should accept the place, as it would mean a drastic reduction in our standard of living, and would certainly put off any thoughts we might have had about starting a family for at least two years. In the Civil Service my salary had shot up in 1973 and I was now earning around £3,000 a year. As a student I would be getting £850 per annum, and of course would have to give up my lucrative tally round. But we were both convinced that the short-term disadvantages would be more than compensated for in the long term, both in salary prospects and in job satisfaction. So I accepted the place and informed my employers that I would be leaving in September.

Once I knew I was leaving, life in the Civil Service did not seem so bad after all. I had got to know and be known by a great many people, and had had quite a lot of fun working there. They had a collection for me throughout the building, and the cheque when it was handed to me was quite a sizeable one. On my last day I had a leaving party, first downstairs in the bar, and then, just for the girls I worked with, in the office. I was almost overwhelmed by the number of people who came to say good-bye personally, to wish me luck and buy me a drink. Even some of the officers who had left the building or department travelled in to give me their personal wishes. When I eventually staggered back upstairs I was in a highly emotional state, and the worst part was still to come. I finally said my farewells in the office, and with a tear in my eye and a huge lump in my throat I made my way down to the station trying desperately not to cry. I had hated the work but the people were lovely.

As the date to leave drew near my old feelings of insecurity and self-doubt had returned. I had been in the same job for over six years. I was safely established in a routine, I was popular amongst the people with whom I worked and more than confident that I could do the job. Now I was off to start a course about which I realised I knew very little. I was to be mixing with people who had been working as social workers for years. At the interview I had been very confident that I could cope with the physical mobility necessary to visiting clients in their own homes—but could I cope? I had felt sure that I could deal with other people's emotions without getting emotionally involved myself—but would I be able to deal with them? I had felt certain that I could meet the challenge of the academic work—but was I really that certain?

Chapter 6

The Student Life

To say that I was disappointed by my first few weeks at the Polytechnic would not be strictly true—I was more disillusioned. I had been expecting my fellow students to be responsible, mature, capable people possessing very few hang-ups and certainly no problems which they couldn't handle. Instead most of them appeared to be very sad individuals who had so many problems that they barely had time to think of other people's. Some of them seemed to be mainly preoccupied either with smoking pot, getting drunk as often as they could, or entering into "relationships" with other students. Other students seemed to opt out of the course from the very beginning, and appeared in college only on rare occasions to hand in essays or see their tutors. But most off-putting of all were those who appeared to hate social work, and made no bones about the fact that the only reason they were on the course was to obtain a qualification and thus command a higher salary when they returned to work. In my naiveté, I had taken for granted that all the students would be as anxious to learn as I was.

My jaundiced view of the first few weeks was of course coloured by my own feelings of anxiety about my position as the only blind student amongst eighty-eight on the course. College was so different from school, and it took me a long time to get used to the fact that it was not compulsory to attend all (indeed any) of the lectures. A partially sighted friend and I felt almost guilty if we missed one class, and certainly we should have earned any award for attendance during the two years, even if we didn't understand half of what was said.

I still had my problem of being unable to stay awake during classes. After only a few minutes of droning lecture my eyes would close and my head would begin to nod. It got so bad at one time that several of the students used to run a sweepstake on when I would actually lose consciousness. Two friends used to seize the opportunity to steal and eat my sandwiches, much to the amusement of everyone else. And one day I surpassed myself by falling off my chair in the middle of a lecture. I just managed to catch my tape-recorder before it and I hit the floor. Without my recorder I do not know what I would have done. It did not go to sleep and I was thus able to play the lectures back at home and take notes there. But I was surprised to find just how much of the information I had in fact absorbed even when I was apparently asleep, and I remember once or twice asking a pertinent question, much to the amazement of all around who thought I was out for the count. When at last I realised that dropping off to sleep was something I could not combat, I decided to send my tape-recorder to the lectures and make a good job of sleeping by stretching out in a comfortable chair in the lounge.

Apart from the practical difficulties of studying I had also to cope with a degree of character analysis (some self-inflicted and some imposed by my fellow students) which I had not bargained for. I realised early on, for example, that I had very few opinions of my own and tended more often than not to trot out the "latest view" as summarised by the BBC news. I knew what was happening around the world, but nobody had really asked me why I thought it was happening, or indeed what I thought at all. I realised just how hampering my lack of sight was, in that I was unable to read any variety of interpretations of a particular theory or model. I also became aware just how susceptible society was, and especially the blind, to influence from the press and television. I began to listen to blind friends talking about football, for example, and to notice how they put forward other people's opinions about a goal or the merits of a player as if it was their opinion. One friend repeated almost word for word what a television commentator had said about a match.

It seemed that almost for the first time other people were actually listening to what I had to say, and after my initial fear of expressing my ideas in public, I became more able to think through a problem for myself and present my own attitude in a rational and clear manner. I learned to answer questions and argue a point, both skills which hitherto I had not developed. One hard lesson I learned was that I had to listen more and talk less, which was particularly difficult for one who had always had more than his fair share of verbal ability.

As the weeks went by and my confidence increased, so too did my understanding and tolerance of my fellow students. I began to enjoy college and to revel in the intellectual stimulation which had for so long been denied me. College also highlighted aspects of my character which I did not like very much. I found that in many ways I was a very rigid person, who tended to see things as either black or white and had yet to learn to recognise shades of grey. I noticed too that I tended to be impatient with people if they did not grasp something as quickly as I did, or if they failed to do anything for themselves to solve their own problems.

But the real test, I knew, was still to come. In February 1975 I started my first practical placement as a student social worker in a local authority social services team in Tower Hamlets. I was immensely worried about how I would handle clients in the flesh and, more importantly, how clients would handle me. So I was surprised and gratified when the majority of my clients received me better than had most of my colleagues. For many of my colleagues it was difficult at first to think of me as a colleague, for their only experience of blind people was as clients; while for the clients, my blindness was in some way a plus, it helped put them at ease.

The practical side of the work I managed quite well. Once I had learned the basic geography of the area, locating particular estates or blocks of flats was no problem. One piece of luck that came my way was that most of my visits were to council flats which had the flat numbers in raised figures on their letter-boxes or doors. I was embarrassed one day, however, when someone opened the door just as I was feeling their number. But once I had explained, the woman relaxed and put the dog back on its leash. And an especially helpful feature of the East End was the vast number of truants who always seemed to be around the streets when I was visiting. I could guarantee that no matter what time of the day I was out I could always find a kid who should have been in school, to show me where I wanted to go. Indeed, when I became better known, the kids used to ask me whether I was coming that way again the next day and wanted to be met?

I also had no major difficulties when I eventually arrived at the flat of the person I was to interview. Some of course were initially taken aback by having a blind man land on their doorstep, fall over the door mat and ask "Can I help you?" But after only a short time I usually managed to convince them that I was just as capable of listening to their problems as anyone else. In interviews I would try to utilise all my senses, hearing, smell and touch. I had been told at college that I would miss a lot because I would not be able to pick up any visual communication in body language or eye contact. I found, however, that once I knew what to look for I could observe a great deal about the people I was interviewing by how their voice sounded, or whether they constantly moved their arms and legs. I could tell, for example, from the sound of someone's voice whether they were slumped in a chair or sitting upright, I could hear whether they were looking down at the ground or at me. I even remember astounding two colleagues by describing the facial expressions of two boys purely from the sound of their voices. One sounded as though he had a permanent smile on his face and the other conveyed to me that he had a vacant glazed look. These descriptions were completely accurate and certainly made me aware that my hearing could be of much more use to me in the work than I had realised. I made full use of my other senses too, to build up for myself a picture of the home conditions in which my interviewees lived.

I could feel whether the settee or chair on which I was sitting was threadbare or not. I could usually tell the condition of the carpet or lino through my feet, and my sense of smell told me whether a place was clean or not. I was particularly adept at detecting enuresis from at least ten paces, and my nose proved more sensitive to the intimate personal aromas of the clients than was comfortable. A bad cold would have been a definite advantage when walking about some of the estates. Frequently there was rotting rubbish at the foot of stairs or overflowing from a garbage chute. Excrement (both human and animal) often littered the stairs, courtyards and landings and I made the mistake of going to work in open-toed sandals only once.

I enjoyed that first placement, and surprised myself at just how well I was able to answer questions and meet requests calmly and efficiently. I seemed able to relate to the clients well and they to me, and the fact that I had been (and in fact still was) a client of the social services myself helped me to put myself in their shoes. I knew what I had hated about the social workers who had visited me, and so tried not to convey any of the arrogance, superiority or sheer indifference which I had experienced. At the same time I knew I had to be careful not to over-identify with the client and thus be unable to help.

One positive advantage which my blindness gave me over my sighted counter-parts was that I had a ready-made excuse for allowing clients to give something back to me. Someone who is forced to turn to a social worker for help has usually had to swallow a great deal of his or her pride in simply plucking up the courage to ask for assistance. Invariably the individual has lost or failed in one of his or her roles in life—as a husband, provider, wife or mother. He or she has also during an interview to answer a great many personal questions and reveal vulnerability, failings or inadequacies to a complete stranger. The social worker is the one with the power, the one from whom help is being sought. While all that remained true, with me the client often had the opportunity (with sometimes a little complicity on my part) to offer something in return, perhaps by helping me to the bus stop, station or street. Sometimes someone I had been interviewing would insist on walking with me to the main road, even though he and I knew that I could manage perfectly well.

I had originally been worried that my clients' feelings about me—their sympathy towards me or scepticism as to whether someone with such an obvious disability could help them— would prevent them from accepting my advice and respecting it. I need not have had any such fear, as almost without exception I found that what I had to say was accepted just as readily as the advice from any sighted social worker.

This experience of recognition was a reward I had not foreseen. I had been striving for many years to get people to accept me as an "equal", and to regard me as "Mike" who happened to be blind rather than as "blind Mike". I had become sensitive to, and able to detect, those people who talked at me purely because I was blind. With some people it was almost as though they were doing their duty, and they made it perfectly obvious that they were not interested in what I was saying. I remember hating going to parties on my own because I felt people were talking to me because they thought they should, rather than because they wanted to. I have discussed this with several of my friends and all admitted to having felt the same at various times in their lives. So my first taste of real social work in action did a great deal to raise my own general self-esteem. People did find my suggestions useful and realistic. They listened to what I had to say and then judged my advice on its merits.

The report on the placement was good and I went on to my next social work experience (as a member of staff in a children's home) with added confidence.

The children's home was a very large one in Camden, with over fifty beds. The space was split into five separate flats, each with its own living, bedroom and dining area. I was attached to the unit with the oldest kids in it, their ages ranging between eleven and seventeen. Most of the kids in the home had been in care for a number of years and looked likely to remain in care until they were eighteen. My work duties were the same as those of any other male member of staff—I played games with the kids, talked to them, prepared them for bed, supervised them in activities, took them shopping. I also had an opportunity to involve myself with the younger children in the day-care unit operated within the home.

My sporting interests were a good link with most of the boys, and it did not take long for them to start experimenting playing football with their eyes shut. Most of the kids seemed to take an interest in me because, I suppose, I was different from their run-of-the-mill "staff". Many learned the basics of braille and enjoyed deciphering the rude jokes or stories I wrote down for them. I always had with me a pack of braille playing cards or other games that have been adapted for the blind. Sometimes I let the kids take me over an assault course in a local park, and I was surprised at just how concerned and aware of my difficulties they could be, and how much effort they made to ensure that I didn't hurt myself. They acted for all the world like cautious parents taking their naughty child for a romp in the park.

My powers of perception, observation and anticipation were certainly heightened and put to the test by this placement. I constantly had to be aware of what the children were doing and I learned to deduce a great deal from a child's voice or the sound of a movement. They tried to test me out frequently, and it became a sort of game for 'them to try to trick me into believing they were somebody else, and for me to try to convince them that no matter what they did I would be able to see through it. They would do things in front of me that they knew they were not supposed to, like smoking, but I always managed to detect the smell or gain some other indication of what they were doing and act speedily. One poor kid seemed to be caught by me several times a week. I would smell the smoke in his bedroom or in the toilets after he had been in there. But after I had confiscated several packets of cigarettes, very few ever tried smoking in front of me. I eventually became so adept at knowing what they were doing that several of them became convinced that I could see.

I had also at this placement to work through some of my own feelings about institutional care. I knew from first-hand experience what some of the feelings of the kids were. The staff were not "parents" and most of the kids had never had any experience of family life in the usual sense of the word. I had to guard against allowing my feelings and personal experiences to block the good and positive aspects offered by the home and not keep comparing it to "family life". In any case, of all the placements I think I enjoyed my time in the children's home most, and I seriously contemplated looking round for a residential post when I finished the course. There were no blind men doing this type of work as far as I knew, but there could be a first.

When deciding upon my third placement, I deliberately looked at the area I knew least about and was most frightened of: I chose to work for five and a half months in a mental hospital. I was eventually placed at the German Hospital in Hackney, which had two psychiatric wards with about fifteen beds in each, and it was with some fear and trepidation that I turned up on my first day. Like most other people, I had heard a multitude of stories about the

93

happenings in mental hospitals and I thought that if only fifty percent were true I would be in for a difficult time. I had visions of every patient being a violent psychopath and imagined myself on almost permanent guard against physical attack.

The reality of the situation I found completely different, and when after three weeks I stopped shaking in my boots I managed to relax and enjoy it. The majority of the patients appeared to be very sad, depressed people with difficult or strange families. Some were alcoholics trying to get off drink and others were highly manipulative clever people who were trying to "work the system". A few definitely acted very bizarrely and occasionally one of the patients would start shouting for no apparent reason, but acts of physical aggression were very few. I did however, find many incidents to make me smile.

One patient, for example, caused me all kinds of problems by insisting on meditating on the stairs. Several times I went racing up the stairs to the wards and trampled all over him. After I had been there only a few days he vacated the stairs and either gave up his religion or found a safer place to take up his cross-legged pose. On another occasion I was mistaken for a patient by a relative of an in-patient, who was waiting to see the doctor in the secretary's office. I walked in to speak to the typist, not knowing the relative was there, and proceeded to walk round the office whilst I spoke. Apparently I put the fear of death into her because, as she put it, I "kept lunging towards her". The secretary had tried to put her right but I am not sure that the woman (or for that matter the secretary) was convinced.

Whilst at the hospital my main duties involved attending ward rounds, and feeding in any relevant family information on the patients I had been able to glean from my home visits, contact with the local social services office or other agencies. I was also allowed to have a limited number of cases which, it was felt, I might be able to help on a one-to-one basis. Much of my help was geared to supporting these people when they left hospital and went back into the community to face the same pressures that had probably caused their illness in the first place.

One case I was allocated was of a forty-five-year-old alcoholic woman on whom everyone—including the consultant —had given up. She had been in twice to "dry out" and had been admitted a third time suffering from "D.Ts". The consultant said encouragingly to me when he gave permission for me to see Mrs. S, "There's nothing you can do for her and you certainly can't do any harm". With this reassuring boost to my confidence I began seeing her twice a week, and discussed first her family problems and then her drinking. Since I had a limited number of cases, I was able to work at a relatively leisurely pace and certainly in greater depth than usual. But once I gained the trust of the patient I had to know what to do with it. Mrs. S. said that she did want to give up drinking for the sake of her eight-year-old daughter, because she recognised that if she carried on as she had been, her daughter would more than likely be taken into care by the local authority. But I had learned how easy it was to want to do something for the wrong reason, and knew that it was important for Mrs. S. to give up drink for her own sake. She was already in bad health and had lost some of the movement of her right arm. It seemed that her husband had died suddenly eighteen months earlier, and she had started drinking a couple of years before his death. I met her family, including her elder daughters, son-in-law and own sister, and for a time up to Christmas it appeared that she was winning and had not had a drink. At Christmas, unfortunately, she slipped back and spent almost the whole time unconscious. I had expected a relapse, and began again to work with Mrs. S. and her family to try and build up some basic support outside the hospital to help her beat the demon.

Some two-and-a-half months after Christmas I left the placement and crossed my fingers and hoped that Mrs. S. and her family would be strong enough to cope. I had not done a great deal, except perhaps to allow Mrs. S. someone to talk over her problems with who would not judge her. I have since learned that Mrs. S. has remained dry for at least four years. The thought that Mrs. S's. daughter has had four years more of mothering remains a source of real satisfaction to me, though I have no way of knowing how much I helped, if at all.

Working with Mrs. S. and the other patients made me realise how much more there was to "social work" than I had thought. I learned how one's own life experience can be useful, but that it cannot be used as an example or as a model. I learned too, that there was still a great deal I had to learn about people, and most of all about myself. And I passed the placement with flying colours.

For my final placement, I chose something completely different: detached youth work. Most of this time I spent visiting youth clubs, talking to kids on the streets and in entrances of flats. I helped out in an Intermediate Education Centre, which was largely for children aged between eleven and fifteen who had dropped out of school education. As a project I had to arrange and lead a party of teenagers to visit Denmark and Germany. The first two of these activities I enjoyed immensely, but the less said about the trip to Denmark the better. I managed to raise about £2,500 to take twenty-five adolescents from the area for a football tour, and all those involved worked quite hard to raise the money: among the fund- raising activities we organised was a sponsored walk over the bridges of the Thames while I and several others canoed under them. Despite the fact that one of the party announced as the coach was leaving that he did not have a passport, the party set off on time, but little else went off as planned. The trip had been billed as a football educational visit, and whilst the football was not too brilliant the trip was certainly educational, especially for me. I learned the hard way that you cannot throw twenty-five young people together on unfamiliar ground and expect them to become a "group". I also learned that you cannot assemble a group of adults and expect them to "lead" others. Despite the problems however all the party returned home safely and I am sure that all its members gained a source of anecdotes for life. As the years go by, I hope I will forget the fight between one of our players and a Danish player plus the referee! Similarly, I still wake up in a sweat at the memory of us all nearly getting arrested on our return journey for trying to smuggle pornographic literature behind the fire extinguisher in the coach.

This trip, coming as it did right at the end of the course, summed up generally my feelings for the whole two years. I had had a lot of fun, many anxious moments and had, on the whole, worked pretty hard. Where to from there, however? The next task would not be a placement, but a real job, and I would not be a student but a qualified social worker.

Chapter 7

Sport for All

Despite the hectic programme of the past two years, I had also been able to expand my sporting interests: I had added some new sports to my repertoire, and that of our club. The first of these, cross-country skiing, I had been introduced to in 1974, before I got to college, and since this is the sport which I have particularly made my own, and which has probably provided me with more fun and excitement than any other, I shall deal with it in a chapter by itself.

Whilst at college, I also renewed acquaintance with ice-skating, which I had first learned when at Pembridge Place Secretarial College. This sport is reasonably easy once you have acquired the basic principle of balance, and learned how to turn and stop. The biggest difficulty is really in finding a place to skate. We simply went to the nearest ice-rink and joined the hurly-burly among the sighted skaters. For a blind skater, the guidance of a friend is all the help that is necessary: some skate completely on their own, with the guide merely telling them to turn left and right; others hold hands with their partner. This can cause some raised eyebrows if both skaters happen to be men, and at first the officials at the rink came running up in case we might be a cause of trouble. But when they realised our problem they took a great deal of trouble to ensure that we were given space, and were not bothered in any way. Indeed, when on occasion I or one of my friends did not have anyone to guide us, one or other of the officials would lend their services.

One of the new sports I was introduced to was lawn bowls. I was surprised to learn that over 1,000 visually handicapped people in Britain play bowls, and after trying it for myself I could understand why. The rules of the game are the same as for sighted bowlers, but there are adaptations. Generally, the blind bowler will have a small rubber mat placed in the centre of one end of the green. He uses this mat as a location point, and sometimes a very thin piece of string is stretched directly down the centre of the green as a further aid. The jack is then bowled and centred in the middle of the green, and a sighted helper announces its distance from the bowlers: e.g. 28 metres. The blind bowler then knows how to select his wood and calculate the correct amount of force and bias. He bowls, and when the wood stops the sighted helper will call out where the wood is in relation to the jack, using a clock system. That is, the jack is imagined as the central point of a clock and the position of the wood is related to that point: if it stops three feet to the left of the jack but parallel with it, the caller says, "three feet at nine o'clock"; if the wood curls past the jack and ends up immediately behind it, he will shout "two feet at twelve o'clock". The blind bowler thus knows how much he should adjust his next wood to bring him nearer to the jack or, if he wishes, to hit his opponent's woods out of the way. If both players are blind they can both use the same helper. But bowls is one sport where the practised blind bowler can compete in sighted bowling clubs around the country.

I also tried ten-pin bowling, when a student, but I was a dismal failure at it. Several of my totally blind friends perform remarkably well in the bowling alley, but I am afraid to say that I hold the club record for scoring only one in ten frames, a feat which I am told is extremely difficult. My initial problem was that I had learned to bowl in a mini lane at a seaside amusement arcade. This lane sloped upwards and had the pins at the top. Nobody told me that the "proper" lanes do not slope, and when I threw my first ball down the lane and it bounced 15 feet down, worried looks appeared on my friends' and the officials' faces. When the second ball crashed into the adjoining lane several people rushed to give me instruction (and to prevent me from bowling again). But even once my error about the lane had been pointed out I fared no better.

I took my direction and position from the centre of the lane and used tapes as a marker, but persistently swung the ball across my body and bowled it into the gully. I think my highest score ever was 50 in ten frames, and while I enjoyed myself I decided that I would hang my bowling ball and overshoes up, and look for something more spectacular.

It was this, my failure at bowling, that led me to try judo, and apart from skiing I think this remains the sport which I most enjoy. It is particularly suitable for blind people because it is a very tactile sport and requires you to anticipate your opponent's body movements by touch. I learned judo in a class for fully sighted students, and found that my lack of sight placed me at little or no disadvantage. In many ways I was at a distinct advantage, since my reactions and ability to feel body movement were already better developed than those of many of my colleagues. Also for ease of instruction I was used as the demonstration victim, so that I could feel at first hand the position that the thrower should stand in. After some initial embarrassment, my instructor got used to my asking to feel him, and to my groping his legs, buttocks, arms and hips. The advantage in being the "demonstrated upon" also included plenty of opportunities to practise my break-falls. In fact, I flew through the air so often and so high that I began to wonder whether I had wings.

Eventually, I entered my grading at another club and won my green belt in open competition. At the beginning of each contest, the adjudicator would declare that I should be treated in the same way as everyone else. Initially some contestants were a little reluctant to do this, but after I had thrown them or gone for a stranglehold they lost any sympathy for me and got stuck in. Partly because judo was a sport I could perform not only together with but also on equal terms with sighted people, I have obtained a great deal of pleasure (and some bruises) from it.

The other sport I took up while at college was perhaps the least likely for a blind sportsman. This was fencing. An Australian fencing master had approached my club and asked whether anyone would like to have a go at fencing, and a few of us decided to try. Having considered the three basic forms of fencing—with epees, sabres and foils—we finally selected foils as being the most likely to work, as with the others the target area was much too large and required too much guarding. With foils only the trunk of the body is the target so there is a much smaller area to defend. I was shown how to lunge, parry and so on and reasonably soon I was able to fence a bout with the instructor and at least make him break sweat.

After fencing for some time, I began to think how I could improve my chances. One difficulty was knowing the confines of the fencing piste, so I bought some marking tape and marked out the area with the tape, so that I could feel the raised border through my feet. Another disadvantage was not knowing where my opponent was. I therefore purchased a small bleeper which my opponent attached to the bib of his fencing mask. Now I knew where he was and the height and direction of the scoring point. These simple additions enabled me to compete on much more equal terms, and when I joined a sighted fencing class I found I was able to hold my own amongst, and sometimes to beat, sighted fencers who had been fencing for between three and nine months.

My main remaining difficulty was in knowing where my opponent's foil point was when the blades were not engaged; occasionally opponents would stand at the back of the piste and then run at me. So I asked an electronic-minded friend to make a foil which bleeped, and surprisingly this was not difficult to do. He used an ordinary electric foil, took the button off the tip and simply replaced it with a minute speaker. This was connected through the wires in the blade to a power pack and oscillator which plugged into the handle of the foil. The battery and oscillator were then put into the jacket of the user of the adapted blade. If my opponent used this blade I could tell where his blade was at all times and rule out any sneaky form of attack.

I managed eventually to obtain my bronze fencing award and became, as far as I am aware, the first totally blind person in Britain to do so. But much as I enjoyed my fencing I was aware that it did require a great deal of complicity on my opponents' part. They had to agree to wear the bib bleeper and use the adapted foil; and occasionally the bleeper failed. After a time I began to feel that this was a sport that could not be further developed for the blind.

During my last year at college, I had to do a special project on some subject loosely related to social work, and the subject I chose was sport and the disabled. My study was to cover the history of sport for the disabled, with special emphasis on its psychological and emotional significance. I knew that for me, sport was a unique opportunity to test myself, to show both myself and others what I could do. In a sense it was a therapy, a means whereby I could show myself that I could master aspects of my disability, that achievement remained dependent on my own effort- "disabled" need not mean not able. And it was also in another sense a political act, a demonstration to others of being able. Now I wanted to discover what sport meant to other disabled people.

My first problem was to define what for purposes of the study I meant by "disabled". A dictionary definition of the word "disable" did not help much: "to make unfit (physically), incapacitate, deprive of power of action, to injure, cripple" (Universal Dictionary). This was much too broad for my purposes, as it included everyone with a handicap. Someone with a stutter, for instance, is hardly "disabled" as far as sport is concerned. So I decided to restrict my survey to people who were totally blind, had limbs amputated or suffered specifically from spasticity, muscular dystrophy, spina bifida or cerebral palsy. I found that there was a wide range of sports done by this group of people, both competitively and purely for pleasure. I decided to focus on competitive sport.

When researching the history of competitive sport for the disabled, one inevitably starts at the Stoke Mandeville Sports Stadium in Aylesbury, Bucks. This is a memorial to the work of a distinguished former surgeon at the Stoke Mandeville hospital, which specialises in the treatment of spinal injury. The name of the surgeon is Sir Ludwig Guttmann.

Ludwig Guttmann came to this country in the late 1930s, in order to escape Hitler's persecution of the Jews. He was a brilliant surgeon, and during the war he pioneered revolutionary new treatments for spinal injuries at Stoke Mandeville, which undoubtedly saved the lives of many hundreds of men, many of them airmen injured when their planes crashed. His work has earned him world-renown, and in 1969 a knighthood.

Dr. Guttmann was very well aware that, as well as medical treatment for broken bodies, these newly disabled young men needed psychological and emotional help. Something had to be done to combat the boredom of long hospitalisation and the drain on self-confidence that permanent disablement involved. So he decided to see what sport could accomplish. He started his patients on archery and a few other field events, and was so impressed with their performances that he decided to stage a small competition with sixteen paraplegics (fourteen men and two women) all of whom were, or had been, patients at Stoke Mandeville. These games were held in 1948 and proved so popular and successful that they inaugurated an annual competition known as the "Stoke Mandeville Paraplegic Games". The range of events and the levels of performance achieved by these disabled athletes soon became well known throughout the world, and Dr. Guttmann and a few of his sportsmen were asked to travel abroad to demonstrate what sports were possible and how they were done. As enthusiasm for disabled sport spread around the world, the first "International Paraplegic Games" were held in Rome in 1960. This city was chosen because it was the venue for the Olympic Games the same year and it was felt that a time when sport was receiving such international coverage would be a perfect opportunity for publicising the fact that sport need not be exclusive to the able-bodied.

These games have been held annually since 1960. Except in every fourth year, when they are held in the host country for the Olympics, they are held at Stoke Mandeville. The Disabled Olympics, as they are now known, have so far been held in Rome in 1960; Tokyo in 1964; Israel in 1968 (when the venue for these games should have been Mexico, but the authorities there said that they could barely cope with able-bodied athletes let alone disabled ones); Germany in 1972; and Canada in 1976.

The Stoke Mandeville Games up to 1961, and the International Games up to 1973, were for paraplegics only. But Sir Ludwig worked hard for the inclusion of other handicaps, and in 1961 the British Sports Association for the Disabled (B.S.A.D.) was formed, with Sir Ludwig as its President. The B.S.A.D. is the body recognised by the Government as responsible for the provision of sport for all disabled, and in order to meet their new responsibility the Stoke Mandeville Paraplegic Games became the Stoke Mandeville Multi-disabled Games. This important change meant that amputees, the blind, spastics and several other disabled groups could take part. The disabilities included in the international games did not expand until 1974, and the games held in Canada in 1976 were the first truly "Disabled Olympics", with entry open to paraplegics, blind and amputees. In 1980 the Arnhem Games will be open to Cerebral Palsy athletes as well.

As publicity and interest in disabled sport has grown, so too has the number of handicapped competitors. At the Stoke Mandeville Games the number has risen from 16 in 1948 to over 900 in 1975, divided into two classes, junior and senior. In the

International Games that I attended at Stoke Mandeville in July 1975 there were 630 competitors from over 33 countries, including such unexpected co-competitors as Israel and Egypt, the U.S.A. and Poland, Korea and India. At the 1976 "Disabled Olympics" over 1,100 paraplegics and over 600 blind or amputees competed, with entries coming from 60 countries.

The B.S.A.D. headquarters are at Stoke Mandeville, and as well as a general administrator and secretarial staff the association has technical officers whose task it is to visit schools for the disabled, clubs and sports centres, to advise on techniques for particular sports, to help in training and to demonstrate specialist equipment.

Over the past few years the B.S.A.D. has set up a number of regional committees whose task it is to advise on disabled sport and to give information on facilities in local areas, as well as to act as consultants to local authorities and to organise demonstrations and competitions in their regions.

A recently published report[i] by the Disabled Living Foundation, which has done a great deal to publicise sport and recreation for the handicapped, actually lists bodies responsible for the administration of particular sports, plus details of clubs and organisations all over Britain which cater for disabled sportsmen. The foreword to the book summarises the Foundation's view as follows:

"...if the environment of the disabled is carefully studied (interpreting the word environment in its widest possible meaning to include everything in the circumstances of the disabled from birth to death), then ways can be found in subsequent action to return opportunities in life which have hitherto been lost. Physical recreation in its widest connotation has a part in the lives of everybody, or it should have if we are to live fully."

As the sports movement for the disabled has grown, so too have the facilities opened to the handicapped. In London, recently built sports centres such as those at Harrow and the Michael Sobell Centre in Islington have been planned with full access for all very much in mind. Many local authorities are also helping by building slopes and ramps and installing lifts in swimming-baths and bowls areas to permit access by wheelchair users. The facilities at Stoke Mandeville have also grown. In addition to a 400 metre running track and throwing area for field events, there is an indoor basketball/volleyball court, with banked seating for 200, and gymnasium facilities, weightlifting area, fencing area, indoor and outdoor bowling greens, a 25-metre indoor heated swimming pool, three snooker tables and four table-tennis tables. The complex also has living accommodation for up to 700.

The question is, in short, not, "What sports can the disabled do?", but "What sports can't the disabled do?" The following is a list of the sports which I personally know can be undertaken by physically handicapped sportsmen:

Track Events
Wheel-chair racing, wheel-chair obstacle races, wheel-chair slalom.

Field Events
Shot-put, discus, javelin, precision javelin.

Indoor events
Bowls, billiards, basketball, volleyball, snooker, badminton, table tennis, hockey, fencing, weight-lifting, ten-pin bowling.

Outdoor activities
Bowls, archery, dartchery (darts with arrows), shooting, horse-riding, ski-bobbing, sledging, camping.

Water Sports
Swimming, sailing, canoeing, rowing, fishing, aqua-diving.

Apart from badminton, snooker and billiards the blind can take part in all of these sports, plus football, cricket, ice-skating, skiing, water skiing, running and walking races, high jump and long jump, judo, wrestling, mountaineering, golf and surfing. And I actually read recently about a blind one-legged alpine skier from France, as well as about blind parachute jumpers and glider pilots.

What makes men and women put so much effort into these achievements, many of which must involve considerable physical risk? In my study I wanted to discover answers to three basic questions:

(a) Why do disabled people participate in sport?

(b) What makes them choose the particular events they do?

(c) What do the able-bodied think about sport for disabled people, and what is their reaction to it?

When I interviewed Sir Ludwig Guttman, I asked him to list some of the reasons why he introduced sport to his patients. The prime ones, he said, were to relieve the boredom of long hospitalisation; to improve physical fitness and to increase their awareness of what their new body make-up can do; to give them the self-confidence to say "I'm as good as anybody else" and to help their social integration. All these themes were to recur again and again in my study, as in my subsequent experience of "disabled" sport.

(a) Relief of Boredom

As Sir Ludwig has written elsewhere[ii] "the great advantage of sport over formal remedial exercise lies in its recreational value, which is an additional motivation for the disabled in that it restores that pattern of playful activity and a desire to express joy and pleasure in life so deeply inherent in any human being. There is no doubt that much of the benefit of sport as a form of rehabilitation is lost if the disabled do not derive pleasure from its recreational value. This is of particular importance for many severely physically disabled who, today, are employed. Many of them work in factories or offices and for them sport can have the same beneficial effect in counteracting boredom and frustration caused by the monotony of work, as it does for the able-bodied".

Ken Roberts, himself a paraplegic and a yachting coach, makes the same point when he explains[III] that sport because it involves games is more acceptable as a means of improving physical fitness than the monotony of traditional exercise. Sport is both more interesting, and more enjoyable.

(b) Improvement of physical fitness and physical self-awareness

Sir Ludwig, in his article expands on this point too:

"It is a proven fact", he says "that sport can be of immense therapeutic value. It provides the most natural form of remedial exercise and can be successfully employed as a complement to the conventional methods of physiotherapy. It is invaluable in restoring the disabled person's strength, coordination, speed and endurance. In contests with himself and to improve his performance, the severely physically handicapped patient learns to overcome fatigue, the prominent symptom in the early stages of rehabilitation, and this applies as much to the amputee and blind as it does to the spinal paraplegic and tetraplegic".

A vivid description of the effort involved in mastering a physical disability is contained in Norman Croucher's book Shin Kicking Champion[IV]. Norman Croucher lost both his legs as a result of an accident, and had to go through a long painful adjustment to using two artificial limbs. But his determination to stretch himself was clear when he was still on crutches.

"One afternoon on the way back from the beach, we passed a tree which looked to me easy to climb. I scrambled over a small wire fence to reach the tree and began to climb. I had to do all the work with my arms and I found that if I placed my pylons carefully on branches the wood supported my weight. After a great struggle I rose only nine or ten feet above ground level but an important idea was born; when I had artificial legs I would try to climb".

When I interviewed Norman, he told me that he thought that self-awareness of one's capabilities and limitations was one of the most important, but also one of the hardest things to accomplish. At some time or another, when the individual with a disability is dubious as to what are his or her "capabilities", they should try to contrive a situation which would put them to the test fully but safely, and without endangering others.

In his own case, he was unsure whether his stamina would be adequate for the rigorous mountain climbs, the tricky long walks that would be involved between rests in mountaineering. So in order to test his fitness, and the effects on his body of continued strenuous activity, he undertook a walk from John O'Groats to Land's End. This journey took him three months to complete. The walk caused immense pain and discomfort and blistered and chafed his stumps badly, but he proved to himself that his body could stand anything, within reason, that he threw at it. The mental gain was immense as it improved his self-confidence and enabled him to say and believe, that he was as good as anybody else.

Sir Ludwig says that "Sport puts the fight back into fighters".[v] But if this is so, it becomes very important, as Ken Roberts has pointed out[vi], that the sport be introduced to a newly disabled person correctly. It is no good simply holding up the shining examples of other disabled sportsmen's achievements, because at this stage their attainments look too far beyond the reach of the newly handicapped individual who has no personal standards by which to measure himself.

This is particularly true if the shining example held up was a distinguished athlete before his or her disablement. Beatrice

Wright, in her book *Physical Disability*[vii] makes a useful contribution to this discussion on a different but related point when she says that the fact that an amputee has managed to capture a limbed badminton title in his home town does not necessarily mean that he accepts his disability, but on the contrary, could mean that he has not accepted it at all—his main driving force may have been to show that his limblessness does not matter. In fact it matters a great deal, and acting like a "normal" person does not mean that one is "normal" or that one feels like a "normal" person. The key to confidence is acceptance of the disability, and adaptation to it.

One consequence of this approach is that the form of participation in a particular sport should fit the circumstances of the disabled person: one does not need to cling to the rules of the game just because the physically able play that way. According to Sir Ludwig, "The aim of sport is to develop self-discipline, self-respect, competitive spirit and comradeship; mental attitudes which are essential for the disabled person's integration or reintegration into the community."

He also adds that a disabled person's achievements in sport might have the additional advantage of impressing a prospective employer and perhaps change the latter's view of his capabilities. This, I suppose, may be true, but one only gets an interview after some kind of form filling and I have not seen a job application form which asked, "What sports do you participate in and have you won any medals?"

(c) Social Integration

Mental attitudes do indeed help social integration, and sporting achievement is clearly an aid to confidence. To a sportsman, sport is sport no matter who plays it, and also, in a sense, no matter what the level of performance attained. This is a strong common ground for the disabled and able-bodied to communicate more freely. When one takes into account the overwhelming problem of social isolation suffered by the disabled as a whole, this function of sport can be fully appreciated.

The survey was a small one involving 50 persons in all (25 of them interviewed personally) of whom 35 had been disabled from birth and 15 later in life. Their average age was 30. But their responses have been confirmed by my subsequent experience, and they remain valid for the questions they raise about the meaning of sport to the disabled.

All those disabled later in life whom I studied had become disabled after the age of twelve, and before their disablement had participated in a range of sports: rugby, football, cricket, ice-skating, athletics, swimming and fishing. Since they had become disabled, most of these had tried to take up sporting activities again, experimenting until they found one which they enjoyed and, in general, did best. Eight however said that they had chosen particular sports for particular reasons: five said that they had deliberately chosen not to do sports which they had undertaken prior to becoming disabled, three that they had stuck to sports they had done before. One man, aged 39, I remember in particular. He had at one time been a member of the English Youth Athletic Team in the discus and javelin events. He said that these events now gave him no pleasure at all. He could derive no satisfaction from throwing a discus fifteen metres where previously he could have thrown it fifty, and being reminded of the many things he could now not do. So he had specifically chosen a new sport, table tennis, at which he felt he could do well, and at which he could compete against the able-bodied.

All fifty respondents told me that they did sport for enjoyment; thirty-five said for the competition as well, and ten for therapy also.

After some discussion however, another factor emerged. For some, sport represented the chance to show others what they could do. They regarded the publicity they were exposed to as tolerable because it was a way of educating the public, and improving general awareness that the old conception of disablement as meaning non-competence could be buried in the past. They took pride in showing that they were not helpless, but capable of doing things people had hitherto thought were not possible. Participation in sport, what is more, got them away from the home or office desk, and for some it provided the major source of relief from boredom in daily life. Many to whom I spoke said they were lonely at home, and that sport provided opportunities for meeting people as well as some common interest with strangers.

I followed up some of the above points when I interviewed in depth two prominent disabled sportsmen, both of whom have already been quoted in this chapter: Norman Croucher and Ken Roberts. Norman lost his legs at the age of eighteen when, in a drunken stupor, he fell down a railway embankment and had his legs severed below the knees by a train. Now his accomplishments include authorship of several books as well as many mountaineering successes. He described to me how he had got started at rock-climbing after his accident. He wrote to someone running a training course, but omitted to mention that he was an amputee. When he arrived, he handed the instructor a newspaper cutting about a mountaineer who had lost his feet through frost bite, but claimed that he could climb again. The instructor said that it might be possible, and Norman replied, "Well, I have no legs, how about trying with me?" His perseverance and singlemindedness eventually paid off, and after a few months he was climbing quite difficult cliffs. His main goal however was mountaineering, and it was to test his fitness for this that he embarked on his gruelling walk from John O'Groats to Land's End. Over the past few years, he has climbed Mont Blanc, the Matterhorn and the Eiger.

"Climbing," said Norman, "for me was a saving grace, a straw for survival which I clutched with both hands." In this sport he feels he has found fulfilment in many ways. It has been a test of capabilities, strength, courage and skill; and a source of many friendships and immeasurable pleasure.

Ken Roberts is paralysed from the waist down. He is also the first paraplegic to qualify as a Royal Yachting Association sailing instructor. Thus he takes pride not only in becoming a competent sailor, but in having won the confidence of others as capable of instructing others—those who are not handicapped as well as those who are. "It is not what you have lost, but what you have left that counts," he says.

It was after completing my study, and finding how complex yet how similar are the reasons why a disabled person chooses to do sport, that I began to give more attention to the idea that the sport chosen does not have to be performed competitively, and can be done purely for pleasure and personal satisfaction. Rambling, riding, swimming and sailing for example are all sports which give a lot of pleasure outside of competition, and all are powerful sources of relaxation and escape from the pressures of everyday living.

I realised however that most of my own sports were competitive ones, so I decided to look around to see what other sports I could do purely for enjoyment. My research proved to be a bit like turning over a large boulder: you never know what interesting things may crawl out. Water sport for instance I had not really involved myself in, yet it proved a veritable gold mine of activities which I could thoroughly enjoy and which certainly challenged me.

Water-skiing I found very thrilling. I managed (much to the surprise of everyone, including myself) to get up first time and complete a whole circuit. The second time I managed to complete a figure of eight, and thought to myself "Mike Hazelwood, look out". The basic points of instruction are the same for the blind as for anyone else. You have to get your legs in the right position in the water to enable the boat to pull you to your feet. Helpers, held me at first, so that I could feel what position I should be in. The next difficult bit is allowing the boat to pull you up rather than try to pull the boat backwards yourself. Then once you have risen to your feet the problem is staying there. The boat is pulling you at a fair speed and your legs start to wobble and buckle at the knees. The first circuit I completed in a half crouching, half leaning position and I must have looked at one point as if my nose was skimming the water.

The main problem for a blind person seems to be to work out which side of the boat's wake you are on, which you need to know if you are to steer yourself outside the wake by applying pressure on the appropriate ski. The passenger in the speed boat could have a loud hailer through which to shout directions to the skier, but in my case he didn't so I sped along in the midst of the wake, shuddering as each wave hit me and generally feeling like someone shooting the rapids. When doing the figure of eight, too, it would have been helpful to know which way the boat was going to turn next, as I could not easily feel when I was being pulled left or right, so I could not prepare myself for the change in direction.

My instructor however commented that from his point of view I was an easier person to tow than many sighted people, in that at least I went where he steered and didn't have my own ideas about where I should be going!

A further problem for the blind water skier is the danger of hitting large pieces of driftwood floating in the water. These the boat driver should be able to see first, and ask the passenger with a megaphone to warn the skier.

Surfing too I found exhilarating, and want to try again. The most difficult parts for anyone, blind or not, are choosing the right wave to surf on, and then timing the approach exactly right. I found that I could usually manage to pick an appropriate wave by the sound it made as it broke, but timing my approach was more difficult. By the end of the session however I had reached what I thought were incredible speeds on the board, and managed to get up to kneel on it. I felt that after a few more attempts I should be able to rise into a standing position. Someone sighted in the water with me was a great help, and I think that once a helper becomes practised at anticipating the waves for the blind surfer, there should be no reason at all why he or she should not perform reasonably well. It is certainly something I would urge everyone (whether blind or not) to try!

Sailing is already very popular amongst blind and partially sighted people, and there are several courses in various parts of Britain specifically for visually handicapped sailors. On the two occasions I tried, I enjoyed sailing, but somehow did not get the same thrill or sense of challenge as I get from some of my other sports. Yet I know many V.H. people who rave about sailing like I rave about skiing. Sailing has in fact become so popular that one firm has actually produced a braille compass for V.H. seafarers. In years to come, who knows, you may find yourself on a cross channel ferry, or even the Q.E.2, with a blind navigator!

In addition to water sports, my search for non-competitive outdoor activities led me to try horse riding, abseiling, grass-skiing, skateboard sailing and tandem cycling.

The last of these does not need much description, since tandeming for V.H. people is little different from tandeming for the sighted. It largely depends on the driver and the passenger developing an understanding and efficient communication. Skateboard sailing, however, may be less familiar. As its name suggests, the equipment needed is a big skateboard with large wheels, and a flexible mast and sail mounted on the board. The sailor then stands on the board holding the mast and the end of the sail and, depending on where the sail is directed and how much wind is allowed to fill it, the board is propelled along the beach or track. I had great fun, but found it very difficult at first to gauge where the wind was coming from and how to steer the board. I kept falling off, or overfilling the sail with wind at the wrong angle, and thus blowing the board and me over sideways.

Grass-skiing was also fun, but nothing like the real thing. The ski is replaced by a collection of rollers fixed under a ski boot, and as you roll down the grassy slope you apply pressure with the appropriate foot, to turn in a similar fashion to roller-skating. You have ski sticks to help propel you, or simply to keep your balance.

Abseiling, for the uninitiated, involves descending a sheer rock face or cliff backwards by means of an abseil line. This line, rather crudely described, is a rope suspended from the top of the cliff and passed through a metal winch, or pulley, in a figure eight shape. The person descending controls how fast or how slowly he descends by allowing the rope to pass through the pulley as quickly or as slowly as he wants. In addition to the abseil line, I also had a safety harness which was linked to the instructor at the top of the cliff, who in turn was tied to a tree. The instructor is able to control your descent by reducing the amount of safety cable he lets out; and, for the blind, he has the job of selecting which bit of the cliff face it will be best to walk down. When I tried it, I was also accompanied by another instructor descending by my side, also on an abseil line but with no safety rope.

The worst moment for me, as I think for everyone, was the first step over the brink of the cliff into thin air. You go over backwards, and then place your feet on the face of the descent. Then you lean out, with the instructor taking your weight and controlling the abseil line. When I was standing with my feet against the face and my body horizontal to the road some 120 feet below, I began to walk down. After about thirty feet my instructor told me that he was going to show me how secure I was on the safety line and told me to let go of the abseil line and clap my hands. As I stood there listening to the noise of the traffic ninety feet below I was suddenly filled with panic. Supposing he was wrong, what happened? Whilst trying to pluck up courage I voiced this question to the instructor, and was less heartened by his answer "Then you'll reach the bottom a darned sight quicker".

I gulped, released my grip on the rope, clapped my hands, and then clutched the line again. The only other anxious moment I had was when some loose chippings on the cliff face broke away and I was left scrabbling with my feet. The instructor told me to walk to my left, and I bounced nastily across the face before continuing down.

Peculiarly enough, I found the whole thing a little disappointing. It was scary, but I had thought I would feel more sense of danger and risk than I did. I had also expected more excitement from the feeling of being high up on an exposed cliff-face. Yet, after the momentary anxiety of having to clap my hands, I felt safe and enjoyed the descent. In fact the face we used was not an exposed one—it was in the centre of a large U-shaped dip in the cliff, and therefore protected on each side, so that the wind hardly blew, and apart from the noise of the traffic below I found it extremely difficult to get any sensation of height. It was, in summary, an experience I would not have missed for the world, but, having tried it once, I have no yearning to try it again.

But if abseiling was disappointing, horse-riding (which I had expected to be comparatively easy) proved to be my Waterloo. I like horses and have always wanted to ride—out on the open moors was my fantasy, where I would have the pleasure of controlling the horse myself. On an outdoor pursuits holiday in Devon I had my wish, when we managed to book up some riding at stables on Exmoor. Amongst our group there were several novices like myself and some others who had ridden before, so we were to form one group for beginners and one for the others.

However, there were too many people in the beginners group, and one person had to volunteer to go with the more advanced group. As I thought there couldn't be much to riding, I opened my big mouth and volunteered.

The novices (including my wife) went off first and returned an hour later with smiling faces and a contented glow. They had obviously enjoyed themselves and assured me that they had not gone faster than a walk. I was allocated a large pony named Ginger, and, feeling like Billy the Kid, I swung easily into the saddle. My sum total of instruction was: "Hold the reins firmly but not too tightly, keep your feet in the stirrups and knees pressed into the side of the pony. When you want him to turn left or right apply a little pressure on the appropriate rein, and when you want him to stop pull back on the reins and shout "whoa"

I knew as soon as the instructor let go of Ginger that I was in for trouble, as he tossed his head as if to pull the reins from my hands. He then took me first for a drink at the trough and then over to the fodder area for something to eat. I decided at this stage to comply with his demands, mainly because I couldn't do much else. By the time Ginger had wined and dined most of the other horses had moved off and we were right at the back. I was quite content with this position but Ginger apparently was not, so he decided to speed up and rush through the riders in front like a bull at a gate. He knocked some out of the way and skirted round others until we were at the front behind the instructor. My shouts of "whoa" or "steady boy" were totally ignored, so I had lost round two as well. But once we arrived at the front of the herd, Ginger appeared to settle down and we clip-clopped along merrily. I thought that before we reached the open moorland I should try to form some sort of relationship with him, so began to talk to him in my best social work manner. I told him what a wonderful pony he was and how good he was. As it happened I might just as well have saved my breath.

My crash helmet or whatever they call the thing was a little too loose and kept dropping down over my eyes. It made no difference to my seeing of course, but it was certainly uncomfortable. I daren't let go to push it back on my head and had to try to slide it back by nodding vigorously. After about twenty minutes of clip-clopping and nodding we turned off the road and on to the open moor. The air was beautiful, the sun came out and I felt good. At this point some of the more experienced riders decided, now we were on the open moorland, to try to interest their ponies in breaking into a trot. I had no such inclination, but Ginger had, and when he saw the others kick up their heels, he did likewise. I was a little scared, and annoyed that he had taken it upon himself to trot with not so much as a by your leave: and I soon found that I definitely did not like trotting. When the backside of the pony was coming up I always seemed to be coming down and vice versa. I also began to sweat profusely. I am not sure whether it was heat or fear which caused perspiration to trickle down between my shoulder blades like a never- ending stream, but I had mistakenly put on a nylon cagoule which although waterproof did not allow any air to get to my body or, more importantly, any heat and sweat to escape from it.

I decided after about five minutes bone-aching jolts that it was time to assert my authority. As instructed, I pulled gently but firmly back on the reins and said "Whoa, Ginger". Nothing happened so I again pulled the reins, a little harder this time and shouted, "Whoa there". The only response it brought from Ginger was another spirited attempt to toss the reins out of my hands as if to say, "Who the hell do you think you are talking to?" I knew that if I didn't win the next battle all would be lost, so, nearly pulling the bit through his mouth, I yanked back the reins and yelled "Whoa, you. . . ." This had an immediate effect. Ginger jolted to a sudden halt and

I, pleased with my powers of control, slid up his neck and nearly went flying over the top of his head. He had obeyed me however, and now we both knew who was boss. I urged him gently on again and he calmly and sedately began to walk forward, but I had the most peculiar feeling that he was plotting something. We had again dropped behind the rest and I could tell that Ginger was not happy.

Then, about a hundred yards in front of him he saw one of my friends coax his pony into a canter. Ginger clearly thought he would have a little fun. He gave a massive toss of his head, which loosened my grip on the reins, and launched himself into full gallop. Ginger made up a hundred-yard gap in seconds and my friend told me later that he had felt me and Ginger bound past him as though he was standing still. By this time I had conceded defeat and given up any thought of controlling the beast. He had won, he was boss. I devoted the whole of my attention to staying on the bloody animal. My feet had fallen out of the stirrups, so I bent my legs and put my shoes on the pony's backside, clasped both my arms round his neck and pleaded with him into his ear to stop. One of the group later described me as looking like a hundredweight sack of potatoes slung on the pony's back: all he could see from the rear was my bottom going up and down and my legs shaking. It was all right for him but I was desperately worried about falling off and breaking my neck, sliding under the horse's belly and being trampled to death, or disappearing into the sunset never to be seen again except on moonlit nights when Ginger and I would haunt the moors. The fact that I could not see was probably a good thing in that I was not conscious of how fast the ground was flashing past. Through my terror, I remember feeling very angry with the instructor, who yelled at me from a long way behind- "If I were you I'd slow him down or you'll be back at the stables about half an hour before the rest of us". That was where my sense of humour entirely failed me, and my reply is not printable here.

The comedian of an instructor eventually worked out that perhaps I was having difficulty and help might be required. So he put his own horse into a gallop and came chasing after me. As I hung there with the noise of hooves thundering in my brain I vowed to myself that if I lived through this experience I would never ride again. The instructor eventually began to gain on us and Ginger appeared to recognise his voice and slowed down, knowing I am sure that he had done wrong. The instructor came alongside and grabbed the dangling reins and brought Ginger to a standstill. I was quite shaken but tried to regain my composure and to sit up without trembling. I pushed my riding hat back into its correct position and wiped the perspiration from my face. The streak of sweat had by now turned into a flood, puddles had formed in my pants and trouser band and perspiration dripped from the bottom of my cagoule. When the others caught up with me everyone congratulated me on getting my horse to gallop, and I am not sure to this day whether they meant it or were taking the mick. I offered to swop horses but no one took me up on the offer.

Ginger himself must have realised that enough was enough, and behaved as good as gold for the remainder of the journey home. He tried to trot once but a mouthful of bit soon dissuaded him. Maureen saw us coming from a distance and knew something had happened by my ashen white face and dishevelled appearance. I dismounted, breathed a huge sigh of relief and stood with my legs shaking, and immensely glad to be on terra-firma once more.

My riding exploits soon became so well known throughout the club that I was nicknamed Ginger as a permanent reminder of my ordeal.

Chapter 8

A Nod's as Good as a Wink

By the time I left college in June 1976 I had already been interviewed by Tower Hamlets Borough Council and offered a job as a social worker. They had not however given me a starting date, or told me exactly where I would be working: they were apparently awaiting the results of my medical. I was anxious to get started doing "real social work", and at the same time very nervous at the prospect of establishing myself somewhere new again. I wanted to get the first few weeks over and, of course, to begin again to earn some money. Two years on a grant had not been easy for me and even more difficult for Maureen, who had had to go without many things she might otherwise have been able to buy. So as the weeks went by I became more and more anxious in case something had gone wrong. I was aware that although I was qualified I was still very inexperienced, and I had half expected to have difficulty in finding a borough to employ me. But I had had two practical work placements in Tower Hamlets and was therefore known there. I had also received good reports from both my supervisors, and been vetted by two of the local area teams one of which had appeared to be genuinely interested in me and in what I could offer. I had liked that team. Most of the individuals in it seemed to have the invaluable quality of being able to laugh at themselves and their work. This ability was extremely important to me, as I felt that my, sometimes offbeat, humour might be taken the wrong way by anyone who didn't realise when I was joking.

Eventually I heard that I was to start on 16th August in the Lime house/Poplar area, and in the team I had liked. This particular office in Commercial Road happened to be virtually opposite the housing department building in which my wife worked, so I had the added advantage of being able to travel to work with Maureen in the mornings. She knew a great deal about the geography of the area and could help me orientate myself in relation to particular landmarks and housing estates.

My first day was neither as traumatic nor as dramatic as my first day at the Board of Trade. I was older, wiser, more confident and able to control situations better. But I was still anxious to create a good impression. Deep down I still had the feeling, which I think had been actually cultivated at school, that even though I was qualified I still had to prove to everyone I worked with that I was "as good as they were". This compulsion to prove oneself is something I have been very much aware of since I have been blind, and which many other disabled people had admitted to feeling also. It is as if the disabled person himself accepts that he is a second-class citizen or a second-rate worker, but tries constantly to prove to himself and others that he is not. The slight paranoia I had felt in my placement days returned and I imagined that all my colleagues were watching and waiting for me to do something wrong. I thought that they would judge all other blind social workers from their experiences of working with me. I was petrified of making a mistake in case they said that I had made it "because I was blind", and not because I was newly qualified or inexperienced. This feeling of being watched was pure fantasy on my part and in fact my colleagues could not have been more helpful, understanding and non-judgemental.

At first I had only a few cases, and managed to cope reasonably well with the demands they made of me. The concentration and effort did however have its effect on me and I felt thoroughly tired at the end of each day and totally exhausted by the end of each week. I remember once during that time, on a Friday, going to visit a friend who lived in the Midlands. I travelled with Maureen by train and literally fell asleep standing up in the corridor.

Although by the time I started work as a social worker my general mobility, sense of orientation and use of my other faculties were well-developed, each and every journey that I made or new situation that I faced took (and still takes) a tremendous amount of energy out of me. One of the most tiring parts of my day is still the short walk from Stepney East railway station to the office at Limehouse Town Hall. The route involves crossing one major road and several side streets. Although I have done the journey daily for over three years, I still cannot afford a moment's lapse of concentration or carelessness, just in case a lorry happens to be reversing out of one of the side streets or the pavement has been dug up and a hole left unguarded. One morning, for example, I was strolling along slightly quicker than usual when I found the narrow pavement totally blocked by some metal bars lying flat on the ground. Apparently the crash-barrier (normally at the side of the road) had been knocked down by a car in a police chase the previous evening. I had to walk off the pavement into the Commercial Road in the middle of the rush hour, skirt round the obstacle and get back on to the pavement. That particular road petrifies me at the best of times because of the volume of noise generated by the juggernaut lorries which use it, but actually to have to step into it almost made me ill.

I soon learned that Tower Hamlets is a particularly difficult borough as far as mobility for the blind and elderly was concerned. It is impossible in many of the side roads to walk on the pavement because of the number of cars parked there. Local motorists seem to have adopted the motto "Keep death off the roads—drive on the pavements". Further, nearly all the paving stones and roads are in a bad state of repair and you can never be sure of your footing anywhere. And because of the lack of open spaces most kids play on the streets, so I have to walk in constant fear of falling over an abandoned bike, treading on a discarded tennis ball or somersaulting beam over apex over a skipping rope conveniently tied to a lamp post and abandoned whilst its owner is off buying an ice-cream. Skate-boards posed a special menace, and I shall never forget my first introduction to this sport, when I accidentally trod on a board and shot off down the street performing involuntary feats of expert control and balance. When the kid to whom the board belonged asked me if I wanted to borrow his pads and helmet to have a proper go, I told him what he could do with them and his skate-board.

Other unforeseen obstructions also taught me to proceed with extreme caution. One particularly lethal innovation was the use of diagonal scaffolding on buildings where pavement space was limited. The sections of the scaffolding, instead of horizontal or vertical to allow people to pass between the upright and under the cross sections, are diagonal poles secured to the pavement at the bottom and then sloped towards the building needing support. As I walked merrily along sweeping my stick from side to side I completely missed the base of the pole, but found the upper section quite easily when it smashed me in the face. To say I was shocked would be an understatement and it took several days for me fully to recover my general confidence. I spoke to the foreman on the building site, and he agreed to put a board across the gap from the wall to the bottom of the scaffolding pole and thus provide a warning to anyone like me who passed that way, or indeed anyone else who did not expect the poles to angle inward.

Another situation which nearly caught me out arose when I was walking down a small side street in a particularly rundown part of the neighbourhood. As I made my way along the pavement two voices almost simultaneously yelled at me to stop. I froze to the spot. What was it? Had someone parked on the pavement? Was somebody up a ladder and I just about to knock them off it? Were my flies undone? Having checked the last of these I groped gingerly forward with my stick. There was nothing there. Literally nothing there—no obstacle, no pavement, no road even. As I stood wondering whether the end of my cane had dropped off or I had suddenly grown ten feet so that my stick no longer touched the ground, a child's voice some ten foot below me announced the obvious: "Go back, there isn't any more street left".

Despite these rather disconcerting experiences not too much harm came to me in the early weeks, and I settled into the routine of the office and the social work procedures quite well. As I became more confident that I could indeed do the job I had qualified in, I began to relax more and be myself instead of what I thought others wanted me to be.

My feeling of having to prove myself diminished and I became less anxious to volunteer for virtually anything that was going or to take on any case which nobody else wanted. I was certainly pleased with the reaction of my colleagues to me. Whilst kind and considerate they did not hesitate to disagree with me in discussion or challenge my views if they thought I was wrong. I specially valued this. All too often the nondisabled seem to feel that to disagree with someone with a disability is in some way cruel or unkind. I hate being pacified or patronised, the more so because if you are blind you cannot see the tedium register on someone's face. I have frequently continued to labour a point ages after someone has obviously switched off, dropped off to sleep or even walked away, leaving me talking to thin air.

I was, of course, not the only one to have to make adjustments. There were also many adjustments which my colleagues had to make. One small difficulty for example, which was easily overcome but took a little time, was that many of my colleagues— and indeed friends—did not seem to realise that it was no good giving me a visual response if I asked them a question or was trying to explain something to them.

I remember getting very annoyed at somebody who appeared totally unable to grasp some very simple directions that I was giving him. Each time no response came I would start slowly, clearly and precisely to go through it all again. Eventually he burst out, "All right, there's no need to go over it twenty times, I understood you the first time". When I replied, "Well why didn't you bloody well say so", he burst out laughing. For the previous ten minutes he had been vigorously nodding his head as a gesture of understanding but I, of course, had not seen it. As the well-known saying so rightly says, "A nod's as good as a wink to a blind man". But colleagues did learn to grunt or say "yes" in order to shut me up, although some still pointed at something they wanted me to look at.

My senior had to change his method of leaving messages for his staff, as it was no good leaving me a note marked "urgent" in print on my desk. It might be days before I found it and got someone to read what was written on it. The organisation of the office also had to be changed slightly to suit me. All files were normally kept in the central filing index. But I needed to have ready access to my files in a small area that I could cope with. So my own filing cabinet was obtained, where I could keep all my own cases (suitably labelled in braille) by my desk. I had in fact to keep two filing systems, one in braille for myself and the ordinary file in print for my colleagues and the records. Since I had been a typist it was no problem to type up reports and summaries, but it was a drag to have to write them again in braille.

I also gave my fellow workers a crash course in what constituted hazards for the blind. The choice of the word "crash" is an apt one, as for the first few weeks in the office I crashed into doors which people had left half open, over waste paper bins which they had left in corridors, and into desks which had been moved and not replaced. On one occasion I remember crashing straight into a notice board, which had been conveniently placed right at the bottom of the stairs leading to my office. I was aware that I was the one who had to do the educating, and found doing it in a humorous way often made the point far better than aggression or anger. I informed the erector of the board that I for one had certainly "noticed" it, and would he mind first picking it up from the floor where I had flattened it, and second, informing me what was on it.

Another thing I had to deal with was the annoying habit that many sighted people have, when seeing a blind person walking towards them, of suddenly stopping their conversation in mid-sentence to watch the approach of the oncoming danger.

At college or in the office, two people would often be standing talking on the concourse or in the corridor, and when they saw me, out of the corner of their eye, lurching towards them, would, instead of continuing to speak and thus provide me with a sound beacon to steer round them, decide to stop talking and stand with their mouths open, while I walked straight into them.

In the end, everyone coped very well and after six months I passed my probationary period with the Department and was offered a contract. I liked the team and they appeared to like me. And Tower Hamlets seemed to be able to offer me what I wanted from the job, that is, as wide a range of social work tasks as possible, so I decided to stay. I had trained as a generic worker and certainly wanted to work as one before even thinking about specialising. Here I had opportunities of working with the elderly, the handicapped, children in care, child abuse cases, preventative cases, mental illness and mental handicap, juveniles (some involved in criminal or delinquent behaviour) and families with general functioning problems. Within a few months I had at least one case in each of the above categories, and in addition had begun to help run a youth club for children known to the Department who were considered to be at "high risk" of having to be received into care because of family breakdown, or of coming to the notice of the police because of criminal acts. As well as supervising the kids at the club, I was involved in arranging camping and youth hostelling week-ends and day trips with them.

I was very curious to see how they would react to me, especially when I was in a position of leadership. All of them started by testing me out to find how far they could push me. But it was a revelation to find how protective the group as a whole became towards me if other kids (not in the group) made comments about me—some of the kids would become very aggressive to my critics. But other reactions to me were more complex. I remember one boy saying to me that he didn't try to trick me because I was blind: there was less chance, he thought, of my detecting him and so no triumph in the deceit! One of the boys also gave me my first real taste of having my blindness used as a weapon against me. This boy had got into a nasty fight with another boy. I tried to control him—he became more and more angry and transferred his anger to me. As the row intensified he began to search for a chink in my armour, and ended by calling me all the "blind c 's" under the sun. I was surprised at just how well I was able to handle this and how little it upset me, but it was strange to hear my blindness referred to in any tones other than reverent and sympathetic ones.

Working with the kids, tough as it was, also provided me with some of my most amusing memories. On one occasion, for instance, I was lying in my tent on a camping week-end and happened to overhear two of the boys talking.

One said to the other, "You 'aven't got a mum, 'ave you?"

The second boy replied, "No, but I don't like to talk about it".

And the first boy, after a silence of a few seconds said, "Do you realise, if your dad died tomorrow, you'd be an orphan"?

I didn't hear the second boy's reply, as I was too busy suppressing my laughter.

On another occasion, I was trying to teach one of the boys how to read a compass. After he had been listening silently for about five minutes, he suddenly announced, "I think I understand, if I follow where it says west, I would find my way home".

I somewhat hesitantly asked why he thought that. "Because I live in West India Dock Road" was his reply!

The kids also asked personal questions. One that they and other young children I met in the street often asked was "What made your eye go such a funny colour? It's 'orrible".

When children yelled this question to their mothers in the street, the embarrassed mums would often threaten them with a bashing when they got them home. I frequently stopped and explained to the child and its distraught parent what had happened to me. Eventually, especially once I had begun to go into the local schools and got to know the kids, I found myself with literally dozens of mates to call out to me every time I walked down the street.

The talks I gave in local junior and secondary schools in the early months at Tower Hamlets also brought me many rewards in the shape of help around the borough. When we organised a poster competition, asking schools to submit paintings depicting any hazard to someone who was blind, the drawings and paintings came in by the dozen and we arranged a special showing of the best in one of the public libraries: every possible danger was displayed there, from abandoned bikes and half open gates to dogs' mess and holes in the ground.

Another area of work which held a special meaning for me was counselling the families of disabled children.

At college, I had read many books about disability and its effects on the disabled and their families, and some of them had touched on my own feelings and the problems I had posed to my family at the time I went blind. I began to see more and more clearly just how devastating the arrival of a disabled individual (whether through birth or accident) can be. As hard as it had been for me to adjust, in some ways, it must have been even harder for my family. Only in recent years has my mother really been able to talk about what she felt at the time of my accident and after. The subject still upsets her and she says that she can make herself feel physically sick by recalling some of the most vivid memories. She describes the terrible sinking feeling in her stomach when she was told at work to go immediately to the Metropolitan Hospital, Hackney, because I had had an accident. As she rushed by cab to the hospital she had me, in her mind, run over, knocked off my bike, fallen out of a tree, hit on the head with a cricket ball or shot by an air gun.

When she walked into the casualty and saw me lying on my back with both eyes covered, her legs turned to jelly and the nausea rose again.

The weeks that followed she describes as a living hell. She visited me daily for the months that I was in hospital and, just as I was conscious of putting on a brave face for her, she did likewise for my sake. Emotionally she said the whole experience was like that of a death of a loved one: she had to mourn not my death but the loss of my sight, and much like the mourning period after a death, her feeling was first of anger and then of grief. Why did it have to happen to her son? These initial feelings gave way to immense irrational guilt. If she hadn't been a working mum, and had been at home on that day, at that time, nothing would have happened. Even here the analogy with bereavement does not end, because like after a death, my mother was first inundated with telephone calls, letters of sympathy and visitors when she was still in a state of utter shock. Later, when the reality of what had happened had become clearer and she needed people to talk to or just to be with her, there appeared to be nobody she could approach or turn to. She had many sleepless nights, lying awake thinking about me in hospital, and many days when she could not concentrate and she felt almost permanently tired.

The relationship between my mother and my father had apparently worsened during this period, and I remember asking my mother whether my going blind was the cause for their eventual divorce. She said that the marriage had really been finished many months before, and that at that time they were going through the motions for my and my brother's sake. But the fact was that when my accident happened my father found the whole situation too difficult to cope with, and left all the decisions to my mother. She had to decide whether the doctors should operate, she discussed whether my eye should be removed and provided most of the moral support I needed when I left hospital. In view of the pressure all this placed upon her, she eventually decided that she would be better on her own and some fifteen months after my accident my father left.

My mother had always been the main pivot around which family life revolved. She provided the emotional warmth and stability at home, and she was also the major bread winner, who provided us with our clothes, pocket money and extra treats.

My mother, after my accident and my father's departure, felt she would have to be even more careful not to indulge and smother me. She says that she used to upset herself enormously whenever she had to reprimand me, or deny me something I had asked for. In the early months of my blindness I had quickly worked out that most of my family, Mum included, were a soft touch, as they all seemed to feel they had to give me everything I wanted, as if they had to "make up" to me for my blindness. My mum soon realised what was happening, however, and began to put her foot down. It turned out to be the most difficult thing in the world to treat me as if I was normal and as if nothing had happened; but it was the best thing for me. My mum also had to realise that I was not the only person in the family, and that my mentally handicapped aunt and my brother John also had needs and demands on her time. John had been fifteen when I had my accident, and himself going through the conflicts of adolescence. We had always been close, and my accident affected him greatly, though he did not talk about it much. My disability tended to push us apart for a variety of reasons. One was my banishment to boarding-school, so that we spent much less time together: during the holidays, by the time we had begun to feel easy again with each other, it was time for me to go back to school again. Our lives and interests inevitably began to separate, and he has described to me since how helpless he felt at that time because he did not know what he could do to help most. In fact, he never complained about being neglected by our mother nor expressed resentment towards me for monopolising her time. So perhaps his freeing her to look after me was the biggest help he could have been. As I grew older he played a major part in my teenage years again, by taking me to his youth club or to visit his friends, or simply by involving me at home when his mates came to call. I remember now with much delight being included in the card evenings he had with his friends. They probably regarded me as a bloody nuisance, but John never did. I also remember with much pride the night his girlfriend taught me to jive.

In my own work with disabled people, then, I tried to remember that it was a whole family I was dealing with, and that support for the family as a whole was the most valuable help I could offer.

Most of the work I did with families took place in their own homes, and I frequently found myself in surprising, and at times alarming situations. The most difficult, especially at first, were those involving any threat of physical violence. Not long after I had started at the Department I went with a fellow social worker, who was leaving, to see a family whose case was to be transferred to me. On the night of the hand-over visit we arrived at the flat, to find the whole family of eight were packed into the front room, together with a stranger whom the other worker had not even met. The stranger was introduced to us as Jack and we were told that he was an uncle of the children. Everyone seemed extremely tense, and I could sense them anxiously looking at each other and then at Jack. Jack appeared to be heavily under the influence of drink or drugs (or both). When he heard that we were social workers he became very agitated and leapt to his feet, shouting his view of social workers and what society could do with them. He then began to lunge menacingly though unsteadily towards us with fists clenched, and an evil glint in his eye. My colleague steered me quickly behind the dining table in the middle of the room. For the next few minutes we engaged in a game of ring-a-ring-of-roses, round and round the table, walking first one way and then changing direction when Jack did. We both hoped that it would soon be time for "a-tishoo, a-tishoo, Jack falls down" as we were getting giddy and wearing a hole in the carpet. One of Jack's main complaints was that he had just been discharged from prison but "the social workers" had not found him anywhere to live. As Jack's temper rose my stomach sank and his relations became agitated even further. They eventually got between us and Jack and we were hustled unceremoniously out of the front door. When I got back to the office and read the file on the family I found a reference to Jack, who had been described by a doctor as "a dangerous psychopath".

On another occasion I was paying a routine visit one evening on a family with a variety of problems. I arrived at the house at about 8.00 p.m. and was admitted by one of the two children. This eleven-year-old 'boy had been the subject of a non-accidental injury inflicted by his father, and his elder sister was in our care. When I entered the front room the boy's mother said "hello", and then began to speak in a very strange manner. Just then the boy's father returned, and explained that he had been trying to get a doctor from the local mental hospital out to see his wife because, he thought, she was having an attack of her frequent bouts of mental illness. His wife, hearing this explanation, grew extremely angry and said that his alcoholism was the cause of her being ill and she could not cope with him anymore. She began to work herself up into a raging temper, screaming at her husband. I, at that point, was seated between them and kept looking from one to the other, in the vain hope of intervening in one way or another. But I could not get a word in edgeways, and for once in my life was actually out-talked. As the two argued, it was as if I was not in the room and I sat there feeling very uncomfortable. I heard myself uttering the standard phrases from the regulation issue "Book of social work stupid phrases, platitudes and inept remarks". I started with "Can we talk about this?" and proceeded as far as "If you would just calm down I am sure we can sort something out". The couple obviously had their own ideas about this however, and the woman eventually rose to her feet and hit her husband over the head with a milk bottle that happened to be near at hand. Fortunately, the bottle did not break, and fell to the floor out of reach. The woman next threw a tea cup and saucer which missed her husband but hit me, spilling cold tea over my head and down my shirt. When the tea was followed by the woman herself, who had been knocked halfway across the room by her husband, I knew things were out of hand. I tried to stand and place the woman back on her feet. But by the time I was vertical the boxing match had switched to wrestling with the woman flat on her back on the settee, her husband on top of her and the little boy somewhere in the middle. The little boy was very distressed at this point and was desperately trying to save his mother from his father's beating. It was I suppose, somewhat of a catch-weight contest as she weighed about eight stone and her husband about fourteen. With the sound of fist on flesh, teeth sinking into skin and high- pitched screams from all, I decided that I would either have to run out and get the police (mainly to remove the child in case he got hurt) or intervene myself, and remove the boy. As the police in the district had never been keen to involve themselves in matrimonial disputes, and the child could be battered or dead by the time they arrived, I reluctantly decided to take the second course of action and joined in the contest. I went over to the writhing mass on the settee, located the man and tried to pull him off. He resisted, so not particularly gently I twisted his arm up his back and found that this had some effect. He got up, and with his arm still in an arm lock I tried to reason with him. But it is difficult to conduct an interview with a man in an arm lock, and in any case not a technique taught on the social work training course. I said that I thought it was better that the boy came with me to one of our children's homes until the family problems had been sorted out. The man calmed down a little and agreed that his son should go. I asked the boy to pack his night things, and when he had done so I released his dad, and he and I went out the front door. I told the father where I was taking the child and said I would visit the following day. I heard later that round two of the fight had begun shortly after I left.

At the time of writing this book, I am still working in the same area. As I am now one of the more experienced workers, my cases all tend to be complex or to need close monitoring. I still enjoy the job immensely and still have the good fortune of actually looking forward to going to work each day. But although work now takes up a great deal of my energy and spare time (I often have to work late in the evenings), I still manage to pursue my leisure interests including music, hi-fi and reading. I have also added to my list another activity, that of public speaking.

This last came about quite by accident. One day I got talking to a perfect stranger who had helped me across the road, and soon after I received a request from a Round Table group to speak at one of their meetings. I had never thought of myself as an after-dinner speaker and the challenge appealed to me. So I accepted, and duly attended the Round Table dinner. My inexperience almost betrayed me however, for when I eventually rose gingerly to my feet, I realised I had drunk too much in the early part of the evening on an empty stomach. I endeavoured to remember what

I had planned to say, and then to keep control of my tongue and actually pronounce the words without slurring them. If I managed reasonably well, I was certainly helped greatly by the fact that virtually all of my audience appeared to be in a worse state than I was. I inevitably spoke on Sport for the Blind, and despite my condition my talk had a favourable reception.

On distinct advantage of being a blind speaker, I found, is that you cannot see your audience. So I am not put off by people walking backwards and forwards to the bar, rushing up the stairs to the toilet, dropping off to sleep or sliding under the table. I usually ask, however, that from time to time someone in the audience give a cough just to let me know they are still there. The surge of excitement and nervous thrill I get before every talk I still find exhilarating; but I make sure that I prepare every talk, and do not make the mistake of saying to myself "once you have done it for the first time, the next time will be the same". Before every talk I think about how I can present my material better, make it more entertaining or clearer. Then, when I arrive at the venue, I always ask one of the hosts to describe exactly how the audience are seated (at tables, arranged in a horseshoe, straight lines etc.). Above all, I do not want to repeat a mistake I made in one of the big cinemas, where I sat diligently throughout a film looking at the speaker from which the sound came, only to be told afterwards that the screen was about ten yards to the left of where I was looking. Apparently, half the cinema audience had been following my gaze trying to work out what the hell I was so avidly looking at!

As I have grown in confidence and experience I have widened my speaking topics, and now as well as sport include in my repertoire a talk on aids to blind living, and another on what a social worker does. The former talk deals with some of the aids and gadgets which I use in my own life. I take with me such things as braille machine, magnetic labels for tins of food, braille rulers

137

and measuring jugs, watches and timers and anything which I have adapted for myself.

Since my first engagement at the Round Table, I have spoken at Rotary Clubs, Women's Guilds and Mothers' Clubs, Sports Organisations and Conferences, and lectured in colleges and spoken in front of businessmen. The most prestigious and nerve-racking talk was given at the British Embassy in Oslo, in the presence of the British Ambassador. The occasion was a meeting of a group of influential company executives in Norway who had donated a great deal of money to "The Anglo-Norse Fund for the Disabled". This fund was set up on the initiative of some Norwegian friends and myself, to provide much needed finance to offset the high cost of the skiing trips for the blind which I led to Norway, and it has since helped other disabled people from Britain and Norway interested in travel and exchange between the two countries.

Because of the reception I got at my first talk, I remain particularly grateful to the Round Table movement, and became a member myself in May 1979. Association with this organisation has meant helping to raise money for local charities or people in need, taking groups of elderly people on outings and generally involving myself in local community activities.

My involvement in organising and participating in sport has not diminished either, as I remain chairman of my increasingly active sports club for the visually handicapped. We had long felt that it was high time that every V.H. person had the opportunity to participate in a national athletics competition, so in June 1977 we organised (and arranged finance for) the first Metro "National Athletics Championships for the Blind and Partially Sighted". The estimated cost of the games— £2,000—frightened my committee half to death, but we adopted my favourite motto, "Where there's a will, there's a way", and in fact raised the sum quite easily. We held the championships at the East London Stadium in Mile End, and attracted over 80 competitors from all over Britain. A crowd of well over 500 spectators watched the races and field events, on a day that proved one of the proudest of my life. The meeting has become a regular event, and the standard of performance has risen so rapidly that at the meeting in July 1979 no fewer than eight United Kingdom records were broken. The point is that visually handicapped athletes throughout the country now have standards by which to judge their own performances, and incentives to train for the following year. The number of competitors has steadily risen, and in 1979 the championships also included juniors (12 to 16). The response from the schools has also been good, and it will be necessary from 1980 to hold the junior and senior games on separate days to fit in all the events and all the competitors who want to enter. We have fully qualified Amateur Athletics Association officials as judges, and they have strict instructions to disqualify anyone who has obviously not done the event before or who performs it dangerously. The games are serious competition, to a serious athletic standard such as has been absent in sport for the disabled for far too long.

Competing in Javelin and Shot-put events at METRO National Games 1978

Chapter 9

Skiing: My Favourite Sport

Of all the sports in which I have participated, there is one that I have come to regard as especially my own, the one that excites me more than any other and gives me that freedom of movement in the open air I most love.

It all began in 1974 when a friend asked me whether I and any other club members would be interested in going to Norway to learn how to ski. I thought he was raving mad, but when I learned that skiing in Norway was mainly cross-country skiing, and that the Norwegian blind had been skiing for years I decided "anything they can do, so can we". So a few friends and I decided to give it a try, and not without a few misgivings seven of us joined the Beitostolen ski week in Norway, which is held during the last week in March every year. This is a week's ski tuition for the blind, culminating in a 25 kilometre ski race, and was started in 1964 by a blind Norwegian named Erling Sturdahl. He went blind in adulthood, but decided that there should be no real reason why he should not continue to do one of the things he loved most, which was skiing. At first he skied with a sighted friend, who told him when to turn left or right. Then he thought that more use could be made of the basic trail tracks which are made for the benefit of cross-country skiers throughout Scandinavia. So he arranged for a small ski-mobile or snow scooter to go over a set area, dragging behind it a device which looked very much like a four pronged rake. The prongs were in two groups of two, and the points on the rake made two distinguishable sets of parallel tracks. With these deepened tracks to give him some directional indication, and his guide skiing in front giving him instructions, Erling could then complete the circuit with comparative ease. Once having devised a basic system, he wanted to share his love of skiing with other blind or disabled people, and set about raising funds to build a sports and health centre for the disabled which was eventually sited and opened at Beitostolen.

When I and my six nervous friends arrived at the ski resort we were introduced to our guides. Every skier was to have the personal attention of an individual instructor, whose job it would be to teach the visually handicapped skier how to ski! If both felt up for it, they could then compete as a competitor and guide in one or other of the races at the end of the week. As on our first course there were well over 150 blind skiers, the provision of instructors was no mean feat. I was told that most of these were drawn from the Norwegian armed forces, though some were prominent businessmen and government officials, some were even Generals! My guide was a lieutenant in the King's Regiment, and he certainly had his work cut out with me. The first day I spent nearly the whole time learning to stand up, let alone ski. The next day I managed to tackle several quite steep hills going up, but got totally out of control going down. When I asked how I stopped myself he replied, "If you don't know how to, you can't do it." That cheered me up no end and any minute I expected to receive the trunk of a tree between my legs or to go plummeting over the edge of a cliff like a lemming. But by the end of the week I was able to ski with comparatively few falls, and at times to reach quite a good speed.

I entered all three races, even though I thought that I and the organisers were insane. The first one was over ten kilometres and I covered the undulating course in just over seventy- five minutes. I was pleased to finish and did not hear until afterwards that the best Norwegian had completed the same course in twenty-five minutes. As the tracks went on (and on and on) I felt a bit like a tram, fervently praying to find my tram shed over the next hill. My guide skied behind me, when possible in the adjacent tracks. He would try to give me as much information about the course as possible, such as "slight bend to the left, now to the right, long steep uphill section, and then down" and I obeyed either skilfully (on my feet) or not so skilfully on my backside, using what my guide called "my fabric brake". Partially blind skiers ski with their guide in front of them, so that they can follow his movements.

The second race I entered was the most bizarre but perhaps the most exciting event that I have ever participated in. It was, believe it or not, a ski/shooting event, where we had to ski a certain distance and then shoot five rounds of live ammunition into a target. All the guns had sonic sights attached, which were in turn linked to a pair of earphones. The gun was fixed on a range with about a six-inch maximum radius up or down from left to right. As the sight on the gun lined up with the sighting device behind the target, the note in the earphones got lower and when it reached its lowest point the gun was in the centre of the target area. The skier then fired five shots: each shot in the outer ring or off the target altogether scored penalty points. The skier then skied a further few hundred metres, and arrived at another rifle range where the target was a balloon. Three shots were allowed here, and every miss collected a penalty ski lap of 180 metres at the end. The winner was the one with the quickest ski time and the fewest penalty points. In the race I shot very well but of course did not yet ski fast enough, so was rather crushed at the end to realise that the best Norwegian could ski the course, miss every shot and still beat me by several minutes.

On the final day in Beitostolen we all entered the long and difficult twenty-five kilometre race called the Ridderrennet. This race, over more than fifteen miles, required a great deal of stamina, courage and a thick skin. I was proud to be the second of our group to finish, in a time of just over three hours.

Skiing, I found, provided me with the key ingredients I require from any sport. First, it offered me a unique degree of physical freedom, a feeling of space and freedom of movement I don't think

142

I had experienced since going blind. Second, it offered a challenge in an environment and conditions very different from my normal world, and which themselves were as important as the sport itself. And third, it demanded a very high degree of physical fitness, strength, mental courage and ability, in pursuit of which one could give everything in relative safety. Skiing thus gave me the opportunity to find out for myself what my own physical and mental limits were, in a controlled situation.

With guide Rolf waiting to start at the 1979 Ridderenet at Beitostolen Norway

It was one of the proudest moments of my life when I was selected to represent Britain in cross-country skiing at the first Winter Olympics for the Disabled, held in 1976 in Sweden. I trained very hard throughout 1975, and when in March 1976 I and two other blind skiers flew to Sweden I was as fit as ever I had been. I knew that I was not as good a skier as most at the Olympics, but the fact that I was as fit as they were helped me to put up a reasonably good performance in the first race of fifteen kilometres. My time was fairly good, I had not come last and I had done the best I could. The fact that our team had not been able to find and bring with us our own guides made a great deal of difference, because although the ones allocated to us were very considerate, we had only one day to get to know each other and to work out the commands and instructions that we needed. What was worse, one of the guides spoke no English at all. My own guide was a sixteen-year-old schoolboy who, although a competent skier, was very nervous of me and had never guided anyone with a sight problem before. This nervousness made him indecisive, so that when we were approaching a pile-up of people or an obstacle, he would say "Perhaps you should slow down". But I could not make the decision whether I should or not.

A Thames Television camera crew had flown out with us to take some film of the training and racing, to include in a "This Week" documentary. All three of us had been worried about how the programme would turn out—we had all seen examples of films in which the disabled were treated in a patronising and sentimental way. But we enjoyed the company of the television people, and the "This Week" documentary film turned out very well and received very good reviews by the critics in every newspaper.

On the day after my fifteen kilometre race the big toe on my right foot began to swell and I had to have treatment in hospital, where the nurse put so much bandage and padding on it that it was virtually impossible for me to bend my toes (an essential requirement of Nordic skiing). So when I started the ten kilometre race the following day I knew I was going to have a problem. Not only could I not bend my toes but I had a stab of pain constantly shooting through my foot and up my leg. The race was disastrous:

144

I fell frequently, I couldn't apply enough pressure when going up the hills and often found myself slipping back down the hill I had just climbed. I was determined however to finish whatever the cost, and I limped painfully round the course. My time was way outside that of which I knew I was capable, and although I had not finished last I stood at the end of the race in tears. People were congratulating me, but all I could think of was that I had done all that training, travelled all that distance, been sponsored by a great many people and I had not done the best of which I was capable. I asked the team manager if I could be completely on my own for a few minutes to pull myself together. That is the only time I have ever cried after any race at any sporting event, but I realised then why the athletes I had seen on television sometimes became emotional after a race—they too felt overwhelmingly that they had let themselves down.

I had also later in the week to go through the anguish of watching one of my friends take my place in our relay team.

These disappointments, however, have only stimulated my desire to excel at this my favourite of sports.

I became a founder member of the British Ski Club for the Disabled, and am currently their Nordic skiing organiser. In both 1978 and 1979 I led a party of twenty-five blind and partially sighted people (with their guides) to Norway. And I have been selected to represent Britain again in cross-country skiing at the Winter Disabled Olympics to be held in Norway in February 1980. I cannot describe the pride I feel in representing my country at this event, and I hope that I can repay the money spent on me and interest taken in me by giving a creditable performance.

My wife Maureen has adopted the motto "If you can't beat them join them" in relation to skiing, and she has become quite a competent skier herself, though she has said that she would like for a change to go on a summer holiday where the sun shines on the beach.

Mike and Visually Handicapped Team plus guides for 1980 Winter Disabled Olympic Games

Even my passion for skiing, however, was put severely to the test in March 1979 when I elected to enter the Engadin Marathon in Switzerland. A friendly travel firm had asked me whether I fancied trying this very difficult race, and offered to sponsor me by way of publicity for their tours. The travel firm obtained permission from the Engadin organisers for me to enter. In addition to agreeing, the authorities paid my entrance fee. Swiss Railways gave me free rail travel, and my fare to and from Switzerland was paid by the travel firm, together with my accommodation costs. All I had to pay was my guide's expenses. This guide I had skied with in Norway and I knew he was good and competent to lead me. I knew John would push me, but with humour. And I knew he wanted the same thing for me as I did: to do the best I possibly could.

The first thing about the race to frighten me was its length —it was over forty-two kilometres (more than twenty-six miles), and was much further than I had ever skied before. The second thing was not the fact that I was the only blind competitor, and that the total number in the race of over 12.200 (all able bodied) was simply frightening. The fact that everyone also started together I tried to erase from my mind.

Throughout the week prior to the race John and I trained very hard, skiing further than the distance of the race daily. I thought I had enough stamina, but I wanted to see if I could do it under the six hours allotted to obtain a credited time. The course itself did not seem too difficult, apart from a nasty uphill section in the middle followed by an even nastier bit coming down. I knew my downhill skiing was my weak point, and I knew that I could be in serious trouble on the steep fast slopes, especially if many of the other 12,200 people happened to be in the way. One particular slope, which involved a hair-raising descent and then an extremely sharp left-hand turn to go under a bridge (made of concrete over a road), caught us out every time. Someone had rather thoughtfully covered the upright stone pillars with mattresses, and I could not help feeling slightly suspicious that anybody should have needed to think up the idea of covering them. Even with John steering me, and both of us ploughing with our right skis, that is, pushing out and down with one or both skis to make a turn or slow down, we could not get round without ending up in a heap on the ground. We always went very fast, and I said to John that I hoped nobody would fall in front of me. When he pointed out that that was highly likely, my vivid imagination could picture a pile-up of twenty bodies with me at the bottom trying to say sorry. I nearly withdrew from the race there and then, but in the end my pride and John would not let me.

The day of the race dawned cold and cloudy, and snowing hard. It had snowed for most of the night and I was very concerned lest the tracks, which I needed more than most, should have been completely obliterated during the night. I was assured however that the tracks would have been freshly cut that morning for the race. We had a very early breakfast and made our way down to the start by 7.30, although the race was not to start until 9.00. With over 12,000 people all beginning together it was crucial that we get the best place possible. Because we could not carry much clothing with us and we had nobody to take our extra clothing at the start, we had only our racing suits on plus a polythene dustbin liner each, with holes cut for the arms and head. It was surprising just how warm these liners were. By 8.15 there were literally thousands of people round me, jumping up and down to keep warm, re-waxing the bottom of their skis (for better glide or grip), or simply talking about the race, As people jostled for positions there was some danger of having the front of your skis broken off as they walked over them. I, true to form, chose this moment to announce to John that I wanted to go to the toilet. John uttered a few oaths and then led me past many swearing, gesticulating skiers to the side of the track where, in full view of about 10,000 people, I relieved myself and melted the snow. Then we endeavoured to find our way back. We passed again the swearing mass and managed to find our way to where our friends were standing only by spotting a plastic bin-liner waving from a ski stick held above everyone's head.

About two minutes before nine I discarded my bin-liner and placed it on a nearby post. I did some warming up exercises and was as ready as I would ever be. What I was not ready for was the starting signal. I had been assured that wherever you stood you could hear the "starting pistol". Whoever had done the translation from Swiss to English either did not know much English or had a sense of humour, because, dead on nine, a thundering great cannon boomed out across the valley causing an avalanche in the next town. Since my accident, I have hated any kind of big bang and the shock of the gun going off only 100 metres or so away nearly knocked me straight on to my back and added a brown substance in my ski suit! Everyone surged forward, and as I regained my balance I had two ski sticks stuck in me. I began to see what kind of race it was and put my head down and started pushing and shoving like the rest.

After a while the mass began to thin out and everyone around was trying to find the best set of tracks in which to ski. At the beginning there were about 100 sets of tracks, but some were full of snow and had not been recut as promised. I felt a little foreboding but concentrated on what I was doing and what John was telling me. He tried constantly to find other skiers who appeared to be skiing at my speed, behind whom I could tuck myself and thus benefit from their flattening the tracks and shielding me from the wind. John and I had estimated that, with luck, or rather the absence of bad luck, we should be able to cover the distance in a little over four and a half hours. I was pleased to learn therefore that we had covered the first fifteen kilometres in just over one hour, and hoped that I could keep up that kind of pace. The only mishap I had had, if you could have called it that, was when a female skier stopped suddenly directly in front of me. I am not sure who was the more surprised, she to find herself hit on the backside and nearly knocked off her feet, or I suddenly to find myself halted by a soft, nice smelling body about which in order to retain my balance I had slung my arms from behind. I had inadvertently grabbed two rather well- developed hand holds.

She apologised to me, and being a gallant British chap, I replied that the pleasure was all mine. We completed the uphill climbing section very well indeed and arrived at the difficult downhill section that I was dreading. There were bodies everywhere. As we hurtled down to the bottom, John weaved me in and out of the falling skiers, every now and then yelling "jump". This was my first introduction to ski jumping and I hope the last. When he said "up", I sprang into the air and hoped that when I landed there would be nobody underneath me. I arrived at the bottom unscathed but ashen. We had certainly done better than many but I was glad it was over. I thought I knew how the Japanese Kamikaze pilots must have felt in the war. John thought I had earned a drink and grabbed one for me from one of the many hundreds of drink stations dotted along the course. It is impossible actually to stop and drink, so I placed the polystyrene cup in my teeth and moved forward, tilting my head from time to time to drain the black-currant juice into my mouth. Unfortunately, someone in front decided at that moment to stop dead in the tracks. John, who was getting himself a drink, had not seen this so I went straight into the idiot's back, the cup concertinaed on to my nose. Juice spilt down my front, down his back, in my eyes, up my nose and a little, together with thousands of fragments of polystyrene, down my throat. I swore violently and pushed forward coughing up bits of the cup as I went.

After about three hours skiing we arrived at the section before the bridge that had caused so many problems in practice. Again, we did not manage to get down and round, and although I accomplished a rather professional looking side-slip stop, John carried straight on into the sizeable crowd, scattering them and their cushions and flasks. When we finally got down to the bridge it was worse than ever. The little bridge could, at a pinch, allow six people to pass through abreast of each other. There were over 400 of us with the same idea and something had to give. Everyone shoved, pushed, kicked and bulldozed their way through, including me. I had put my head down and barged straight down the middle of the crowd and broken to the front of the pack when I heard a loud groan at my feet and the feel of something soft under my right ski. John shouted that I was standing on a lady. I tried to pull my foot back. Unfortunately, it appeared that I had my ski through the strap of the lady's rucksack, which was still on her back at the time. As I tugged at my ski I put my full weight on my other ski, and this produced yet another groan as that foot happened to be standing on the lady's posterior. I eventually disentangled myself and remember feeling nothing but anger in case the woman had stripped the wax from the bottom of my skis. In any case, I did no apologising. As I got off her, as it were, four men appeared from nowhere and dragged her unceremoniously to the side of the course. If she reads this book, please would she accept my sincere apologies now, and I hope the marks I made on her back are fading.

This incident under the bridge took a great deal of energy out of me, and by the time I had been skiing three and a half hours I began to feel tired. I was also sweaty, thirsty and convinced that I was mad to have started such an escapade. I was still making good time though, and by and large had been pretty lucky. Encouraged by this and with only the last long flat section to go, felt confident of finishing in about the time estimated. My optimism was premature however and soon after we had passed the bridge luck and I parted company.

My forebodings of the early morning proved to be only too well founded, for about thirteen kilometres from the end of the race, all the tracks had been completely wiped out by the snow. They had not been cut again, and not only were there no tracks but the weather had become colder and the slush and slurry had turned to sheet ice. Dozens of competitors were taking off their skis and walking the last few miles in order to finish, but I, stubborn as always, said that I had started the race on skis and would finish it on them. John had to go in front and I had to follow the clanging noise of the cow bells we had fortunately placed on the handles of his sticks. Although several of the spectators mooed at us as we went by, it was a great help to me. Upset, demoralised and steadily more tired I edged my way to the finish. I could not keep my footing on the ice and fell hundreds of times. Each time I fell over it took a great deal of energy and effort to stand up again, and lying on my back with my skis over six feet long on my feet, I began to appreciate how sheep feel when they are unable to get up. At one point I was near to tears and said to John I didn't think I could carry on. He felt the pain I was going through, but coaxed me to go on by saying he could see the end only a few metres off. Both he and I knew he was lying, but it did the trick and I rose again to my feet and slipped on. Other skiers as they passed could see my distress and began to shout encouragement in their own languages. A Swiss man pulled me to my feet on one occasion and said, "Come on 9551, not far now". Eventually I heard the sound of the speakers and the noise of the crowd and I knew that I was close. John swore at me, pleaded with me and coaxed me onwards, and hearing the end in the distance I summoned my last ounces of strength and staggered and slipped up to the finishing line. My ordeal was not to end yet however. The approach to the finishing booths was by means of roped off corridors, and as John steered me into one of these I suddenly felt a searing pain in my groin. I stood there so tired I hardly comprehended what had happened and did not hear John yelling at me that I had got one leg either side of a marker post. My brain slowly worked out for itself that something was wrong and I withdrew my leg and lurched onwards. I got to the box and had my computer card torn off my start number. I had finished the Engadin Marathon. At that moment I felt so totally exhausted that I vowed I never wanted to see a pair of skis again as long as I lived.

Yet everyone was congratulating me and saying, "Well done", and it took me a few minutes to grasp the fact that I really had finished, and done so within the six hours. I had not however done the time that I had hoped: I had taken five hours thirty-nine minutes, because the last twelve easy kilometres had taken me nearly two hours. I felt better when I learned that several hundred had not finished the course at all. Many others had not completed the course within the time, and of those who had hundreds had finished after me. When the final list was produced I found that I had finished in front of over 2500 others at position 9,570.

That evening on Swiss T.V. I also learned that many complaints had been received about the condition of the course, and that the winning time of just over two hours was one of the slowest ever. The time of the winning Olympic skier did not make me feel good, but the fact that I was not the only person to find it difficult made me feel better. I was also told that there would have been very few skiers in the race who had had only had seven weeks' experience on snow in their lives! I am of course, proud that I finished, and also grateful for the opportunity of discovering my own utmost limit of physical endurance. But I don't think that I will be doing that race again.

The Engadin also made me realise that I do not really like competition. Although the will in me to win is strong, it is not so strong that it is the only thing that matters, and I think that is why I will never be "the best" at any sport I undertake. I will always do my best, and that has earned me a place in the team for the Paralympics: but I long for the day when the competitive side of me is completely overcome by my desire to ski purely for fun and pleasure.

Chapter 10

The Sixth Sense

I have long been aware of the paradox that although my blindness has taken away a great deal, it has also given me something. I am sometimes asked, indeed, whether I feel I have developed a "sixth sense". While it is certainly true that my senses of smell, touch, hearing and taste have developed in a way I would never have thought possible, what I call my sixth sense is something different. It is of special importance to the disabled person, because it is the faculty that may most help his or her adjustment to a disability. It is a sense of humour.

Humour is used by the disabled as a defence, as a way of relieving frustration, anger and pain, and as an expression of reconciliation. I have found that humour is also a very good means of communication with others, of educating and relaxing social relationships. I remember as a small boy being able to laugh at most things, and having a reasonably quick wit myself when the situation demanded. When I became blind, this wit was to stand me in good stead as I was often able to laugh where I might otherwise have burst into tears or become so frustrated that I simply gave up. I called upon it not only in the ambulance that first day of the accident, but even when I ate the plastic racing car -that was included in every packet of cornflakes, chewed a milk bottle top that had fallen in my cereal, wore odd socks or opened a tin of prunes instead of spaghetti to put on my toast.

As I got older my humour was used as a means of combating the acute embarrassment I felt when I had made a social gaffe. I did not want people to feel sorry for me. I preferred them to laugh with me rather than at me. And this applied to my own family as well as to strangers. I remember for instance the occasion when I tried to brush my teeth with shaving cream. I took the tube out of the mug and proceeded rather cleverly to squeeze a long sausage on to my tooth brush. I then placed the brush in my mouth and started brushing my teeth. The taste was disgusting, and I spat it out immediately and stuck my mouth under the tap to wash it out. That was my second big mistake. The reaction of the water with the shaving cream produced great bubbles of foam in my mouth and the more I washed it out the more it foamed. My family heard my yells and rushed into the bathroom. Because I was in hoots of laughter they felt able to laugh as well, though I knew my mother was profoundly upset by the incident.

On another occasion, I was visiting my mother some months after I had got married, and decided to wash my hair. I found the shelf where the shampoo bottle was usually kept and found what I took to be a rather strong scented shampoo. I proceeded to wash my hair with it, but couldn't seem to get a good lather and must have used about half the bottle before I eventually rinsed the soap off and dried my hair. My mother and stepfather had gone to the local pub for a drink and I, after having dried my hair a little, walked up the road in the rain to join them. I was aware of a vague fizzing noise in my hair but thought no more of it until I arrived at the pub, and told my mother that I didn't think much of her shampoo. To my surprise she said that she did not have any shampoo, so on our return from the pub I went up to the bathroom and brought the bottle down to her. Everyone erupted in peals of laughter. What I was holding was a bottle of bath foam.

My list of minor embarrassing incidents is almost endless. I have blown my nose in full view of everyone on a train on a bright pink and white serviette, hooked someone's shoe off with my white stick, grabbed a woman's rather large left breast to steady myself on a bus, and sat on numerous laps in tube trains. The greater the level of embarrassment the more humour is needed to cope with the situation. I remember many experiences surrounding the very

155

difficult subject of going to the toilet, a basic natural function which poses problems for most disabled people at some time or another. The hazards for people in wheelchairs are well known, but the blind have their share.

There was for instance the occasion when a blind friend went into a toilet at Liverpool Street station on his own, late at night. He walked around tapping with his stick looking for the step up to the urinal. He eventually found it, stepped up and proceeded to urinate over the weighing scales.

Another time I was out with a blind friend called Barrie, and two other sighted friends. We had been drinking, then decided that we wanted a meal. The only restaurant available was a bit smart looking, but we decided to try it. Then, when we had ordered our meal, Barrie found he needed to relieve himself. We asked the management for their toilet, but were told they did not have one, although there was a dark alley next door to the restaurant. One of our sighted friends offered to take Barrie round to the alley, so they skirted the restaurant and Barrie was placed in a dark corner. But Barrie is an extremely independent fellow, and said that he could find his way back provided we kept an eye out for him when he came in the door, so our friend returned to the table. Then we all — or at least those of us who could see—watched in horror as Barrie, fearing his corner was not dark enough, edged up the glassed side of the restaurant little by little, until in full view of the sixty or so diners, he proceeded to wet the window. The initial embarrassment of all in the restaurant was apparent, but it soon gave way to convulsive laughter. Barrie, still unaware of his celebrity, finished his toilet with a flourish, walked along the side of the restaurant and re-entered. He could not understand what everyone was laughing at, and for a full five minutes we were too speechless with laughter to tell him. Just as his meal arrived the penny dropped, and in spite of a rapidly diminishing appetite and a reddening face, he finished his food bravely.

Many of the most treasured comic moments in my life, and the lives of my friends, have arisen when one of us has been trying to pass as "normal". It is sad that people with a disability are regarded, and sometimes regard themselves, as "abnormal", but it is a fact that most of us do not like to appear "different". So those with mild or not immediately visible disabilities will often endeavour to hide them, sometimes going to enormous lengths to do so. One group of people among whom this is an obvious temptation is the partially sighted— perhaps they can see only a few feet around them, but they do not look blind. One such friend with very limited vision told me how he got on to a train and in a self-consciously "normal" fashion threw his bag up on the luggage rack. He settled into a seat, then found himself addressed politely by the man opposite: "I believe this is your bag". My friend replied that it was not, and that his was up on the rack. The gentleman insisted, so to prove his point my friend stood up and reached for his bag. He felt the rack and was filled with embarrassment: some football hooligans had cut all the cords in the bottom of the rack, and the bag had dropped straight through the rack on to the polite gentleman's head.

Another friend who has sight only in the centre of his eyes was taking a new, sighted, girlfriend out for the first time. He was out to impress and did not want anything to go wrong. He got through the day unscathed until he suggested they sit down on a park bench for a while, hoping no doubt for a kiss and cuddle. His hopes were soon dashed however, when, on finding a bench, he lowered himself beside her and toppled back into the flower beds. He had not seen where the bench ended. Undaunted, he suggested they start walking again, the girl by this time suspecting that all was not right with my friend's brain. At the end of the footpath there was a fork, and my friend, wishing to assert his manliness, guided them both firmly left and proceeded to walk into the river!

Sometimes on the other hand, one may feel forced into disguising a disability in order not to embarrass others. Travelling up to Birmingham once to see my girlfriend, I had got on the coach early and folded my stick up and put it in my bag. I was seated by the window and had just started to nod off when someone else got on and sat beside me. As the journey progressed we began to talk, and as nothing arose to reveal that I was blind, the fact had gone unnoticed by my companion. Halfway up the motorway, however, he looked out of the window and said, "I wouldn't mind having an Aston like that".

This put me in a dilemma. Should I own up that I couldn't see, and embarrass him and me? It would probably put paid to any further conversation between us, I felt, and I could so easily merely look out of the window and agree. As well as feeling awkward I was also flattered that my blindness was not immediately apparent, so I decided on the "look out of the window" approach and said that the car was terrific.

The next forty-five minutes passed in talk about sport, the economic plight of the country and so on, and eventually my companion produced a book and began to read. I, wishing to carry on some sort of conversation, asked him what he was reading. As I said the words I could have bitten out my tongue. Instead of telling me the title he merely turned the book cover over so I could read it. I knew he had done this as I recognised the sound of the book being turned over—it was a gesture I had seen when I was sighted. Again dilemma, should I admit or not? Having looked out of the window at the car I was hoist on my own petard, so I looked down at the book and said something stupid like, "Oh, I've never read that".

The rest of the journey passed uneventfully and when we arrived at Birmingham my companion leapt up and said he was in a hurry to get another coach but would see me on Sunday if I was travelling back. I said yes, but hoped no, not if I could help it. He got off and so did I, making sure that I made more of a flourish with my stick than usual so that if he was still in the station he would see and save us both a great deal of embarrassment on the Sunday.

The week-end went by happily and on the Sunday I was just breathing a sigh of relief, with only three minutes to go and no sign of my companion, when someone hurried down the aisle and collapsed in the seat next to me. "Hello mate, had a good week-end then".

I replied that my week-end had been good, and then my stomach dropped through my boots. My fellow traveller looked out of the window, pointed to someone outside and said, "There's my fiancée that I was telling you about". Was this man thick, totally unobservant or blind himself? As I sat there Erving Goffman's advice to the stigmatised[viii], "Honesty is the best policy", raced through my brain. How could I own up now, though? I took my courage in both hands, looked out in no particular direction and said, "Oh yes, very nice". But my general stare apparently was not good enough, for my companion said, "No, no, not her, the one in the blue".

I had not been a great believer in prayer, but I prayed then.

I turned my head and said "Oh, she's even better".

The coach started up and I prepared myself for the most difficult two and a half hours of my life. We talked a little, but I felt that the safest plan for me would be to go to sleep, which I simulated most of the way. When we eventually reached Victoria, he leapt to his feet, again in a hurry, said goodbye and rushed down the coach to the door.

I emerged from the coach confused and tense. I was flattered that I had "passed" for five hours as "normal", but at the same time angry with myself for putting myself in such a situation. I had been worried about his sensibilities at the cost of my own? Yet if I was honest I had to admit that I had been projecting my embarrassment on to him, and it was really I who could not handle the embarrassment of owning up to being blind.

If that seasoned traveller on the Midland Express Coach to Birmingham should ever read this book, I would like to thank him for teaching me something about myself which up to that point I had not realised: that I was ashamed of being blind, and so my adjustment to my disability was far less complete than I had thought.

That was one occasion when my sense of humour did not come to my aid in time. But at the worst and most embarrassing moment of all, the incident that makes all the other stories pale into insignificance, I am glad to say that it saved the day.

When I was about twenty, I went to stay in Birmingham, with a friend I had only recently met. His parents had never met anyone who was blind before, and apparently raised a string of problems, when my friend announced that he had invited me. Can he climb stairs? Does he need hand rails? My friend pointed out that it was my eyes that didn't work, not my legs or brain, and somewhat nervously they agreed to have me.

The day arrived and I travelled up to Birmingham by coach which, as usual, was late. My friend and I had arranged to go to a party that evening and we were already late, but his mother had prepared a rather special meal in my honour so we had to go to his home first to eat.

My friend, the moment he had introduced me to his parents, rushed upstairs to change for the party, leaving me alone with his mother and father. The splendour of the room and the table setting alone put me somewhat on edge. I had had a good home life, but it was never what I could have called "posh": we frequently did not have a milk jug and used milk straight from the bottle; we never had special fish knives; and though we used table cloths when guests came, serviettes were completely unknown to me. So you may imagine my alarm when confronted with a large oak dining table surrounded by huge carved oak chairs.

I took my place at the table and gingerly groped in front of me. There was my napkin folded and pressed in a metal ring. There was my place mat, and half a dozen knives and half a dozen forks on each side of it. In front were large silver tureens with various vegetables in them, two of which I had never heard of, let alone eaten before. To my right was a beautiful crystal cut glass in which was my wine. There were even small tongs with which to serve myself. My hosts said that I should help myself and I rather bravely said that it would be easier if they served me. I said that I ate most things and would like something of everything. So my friend's mother set before me a large oval platter covered with delicious smelling goodies.

Now if you are blind it is important to reconnoitre one's plate before starting any meal, in order to identify early any items that might present problems. Bacon for example is difficult to eat gracefully. You think that you have successfully cut the rasher, only to find that the other half of it which is dangling from the uncut bacon rind, hits you firmly in the chin. Chops are tricky too. It is difficult to find out exactly where the bone is and which way to cut the meat.

Having ascertained that the meal was neither bacon nor chops, I proceeded to attack it. Following my mother's advice that when faced with a collection of cutlery one should always start from the outside and work in, I found in my hand a steak knife and a large fork. So, in accordance with another rule of a blind person's eating programme, started to search out any cylindrical or round vegetables to eat first, before tackling any carving or cutting. This advice usually works to the benefit of both guest and host, because the blind eater does not end with ninety percent of his

Brussels and peas rolling all over the table and into the lap of the unfortunate person sitting opposite.

I managed on this occasion to spear virtually all my peas and Brussels, and found myself with only my steak left to cut. The rest, I thought, should be easy. I managed to cut a few small pieces, and ate them with an air almost of triumph.

After a while however I ran into difficulties. Nothing was on the end of my fork when I brought it to my mouth. I would obviously have to cut harder. As I leant forward slightly to get extra pressure on my knife, I was aware of embarrassed coughing from mine hosts. I pressed harder still and the tureens and glass on the table began to clink musically. Still all I was getting was a mouthful of empty fork. I pressed even harder, the clanging of the things on the table grew louder and the wine in the glasses spilled on to the cloth.

By this time I had gone extremely red and decided to give up. I placed my knife and fork together on the plate and sat back. As I did so I had a strange feeling of misgiving, especially when something rather wet slapped me gently in the chest. I reached my hand up to my shirt front and almost collapsed in disbelief. My inability to cut the steak was explained, as were the embarrassed coughs of my hosts. I had cut up my tie. Apparently, as I had leaned forward to cut the meat, my tie had dropped into my plate and for the preceding few moments I had been carving up the bottom four inches. Silk threads were everywhere: in the plate, on the table, on me. Gravy was steadily trickling down my shirt front. I am not sure whose embarrassment was greatest, that of my hosts or my own. It was clear something had to be done, so I grabbed the tie boldly in both hands, held it over the plate and squeezed it, saying, "That was very nice, I'll eat the rest later". I laughed and my friend's parents laughed with me and the tension miraculously dissolved.

After that I became a regular visitor in that house, and never experienced embarrassment again.

Chapter 11

Conclusions

The world of the disabled has changed a great deal since I grew up. There are more opportunities open to the young, and there is more support available for their families. But the basic problems for any family into which a disabled child is born, or of which a member becomes disabled, remain the same, and it has been central to my thinking about myself as a social worker, that my particular experience—as both helped and helper, client and social worker—puts me in a unique position to help the disabled and their families through critical times. I know from my own parents about denial, and mourning, and guilt, and the over-protectiveness that erodes the competence of the disabled child. I know how much the parents need support from others, how easily mothers can smother the child and exclude the father, or the father opts out and leaves the mother isolated and despairing. I know how agonising for the parents it is for them to allow their child to take risks. How also taking risks is necessary for the child in order to build their sense of pride and independence.

Many of these problems can be alleviated by good and timely intervention by a professional, if he or she knows how. The parents need support, encouragement, practical advice and, when appropriate, help to look at their own emotions and feelings. Such help for the parents can boost their morale and confidence, and indeed at key moments convince them that they can cope after all.

Even if the worker is available to offer this support, the help has to be asked for in the first place, however, and I have seen many parents coping under the most extreme pressures and yet feeling that "it is something I've got to do on my own". Yet if they cannot "do it on their own" a state of utter panic can set in and the parent request that their child be received into care; or in extreme cases one or other parent can feel so panic-stricken that he or she will actually injure the child.

Remembering my own mother's terrible reluctance to go out and leave me after my accident, "in case...", I make a point of trying to persuade parents to leave a disabled child with relatives or friends, and take a break from daily pressures.

In families where the disabled child has non-disabled brothers and sisters, I try to help the parents ensure that the needs of the handicapped child do not totally over-shadow those of the other children. The siblings of a disabled child can be involved in his or her upbringing and treatment. When they play with the disabled child they provide him or her with additional and much needed sources of stimulation and activity.

Parents need all the allies they can get, yet it is surprising just how easily help of the brothers and sisters of handicapped children can be overlooked.

The wider family also have to be educated about the needs, abilities and prospects of the disabled family member, if they in turn are to help rather than hinder the child's development. There is only too often some grandparent to tell the new parents of a Down's syndrome baby, for instance, that "children like that" never reached adulthood, or that a handicapped child is best placed in an institution because he or she "will never be more than a vegetable". If the parents have not got the support even of their own families, how can they be expected to cope?

Although when I am counselling the parents of disabled children I have to be very careful not to project my own family's experiences on to them, I do let them know that I have been through many of the problems myself, and some of the relationships developed out of the sharing that this involves have become powerful partnerships to help produce well-balanced, happy young adults who, although possessing a disability, can play a full, useful active part in society.

The story of my work with a young couple in my borough will perhaps give a clearer idea of the kind of co-operation I have in mind.

Mr. and Mrs. J. were a young couple living in a new maisonette in the East End of London. Mrs. J. was twenty-one, intelligent and lively with a happy laugh and a quick smile. She had lost her mother when she was a child and been brought up mainly by her father. Mr. J. was twenty-five and the quieter of the two. He loved football and worked as a minicab driver in his father's business. Both parents had brothers and sisters, and most of Mr. J's family lived close by. The couple had one little boy, Simon, aged two-and-a-half, when Mrs. J. gave birth to another boy.

But he was born on New Year's Day, and since it was a public holiday and nursing staff were short-handed and there were no social workers on duty, it was January 2nd before the doctor saw Mrs. J. and told her that her baby was mentally handicapped. Then two days later she was discharged. Mr. J's reaction on hearing the news was one of total disbelief followed by rejection of the child. Mrs. J. had very mixed feelings—the child was hers and she loved it as her new-born baby, and yet it was "different". She was frightened of it and did not know what to do.

She and the baby were discharged with little concrete advice, and no arrangement for support from a local social worker. It is hardly surprising therefore that after only a few days at home she requested that the child be taken back into hospital or into care.

Both parents were apparently consumed with guilt for having brought into the world a baby that wasn't "perfect", and Mrs. J's feelings were made worse when her father told her that one of her aunts had had the same mental handicap, but it was something the family had never liked to talk about. Had Mrs. J. known about her aunt, she could have had a scan to detect any abnormality in the child and then made the choice whether or not to continue with the pregnancy.

I became involved with the family when the child came into care, and was fostered with one of the Council's most experienced foster mothers, who had already had experience of bringing up a mentally handicapped child. It soon became apparent that the natural mother very much wanted the child back home, but felt she had been talked into putting him in care by her husband and his family. Mrs. J's parents-in-law had totally rejected the child. Yet when I talked to them it was apparent that they had no idea what mental handicap was and what it would mean to the child. It seemed that the whole family had had high expectations of this baby at the beginning of the year, and felt that these hopes had been dashed.

The main work with the family was to get them to discuss together, the baby, and the tragedy that had befallen them. If they could work through some of their guilt and fear, they might be able to accept what had happened, and make a realistic decision as to whether or not they could cope. So while the child was fostered I tried to ensure that the J's had as much contact with their son as possible. They visited him regularly and soon began to have him home for weekends. The foster mother talked to Mrs. J. about him, and Mrs. J. could see for herself the progress that the foster mother's other mentally handicapped foster child, then aged eighteen months, had made.

I had meetings with both the parents individually and then with the wider family, including the grandparents and parents' siblings. I also introduced Mrs. J. to a group of local parents all of whom had children with a mental handicap. She started to attend regularly with the foster mother. Mrs. J. got a great deal from the parents' meetings and in due course she felt more able to cope with the attitudes of her family.

Mr. J. however was still unable to talk about his son, and slightly resentful of any outsiders he felt were trying to tell him what he should feel. Only after a long period of talking did he begin to accept the situation as it was, and to refer to the baby as his "son" and not "it".

The next step was to decide whether Mr. and Mrs. J. wanted the baby to come home to them, or to stay in care. This discussion was a long and difficult one, but because most of the emotional aspects had already been worked through, the difficulties and reservations were now expressed mainly on the practical level. Would the baby need special housing or nursery facilities? When he was older would he need to go to a boarding school?

The grandparents asked me "How long has he got?" Many of these points I was able to clear up, whilst at the same time, the contact between the parents and the baby was continuing. "Make your mind up time" for the family came in August, because the foster mother was going on holiday, so I asked whether Mr. and Mrs. J. felt they could have the baby home for a two-week period. They accepted readily and both the foster mother and I guessed that unless anything untoward happened, the baby would not return to the foster home. We proved to be right, and now some two years later Brian (as they eventually named the baby) is a happy integral part of the family. The foster mother was asked to be godmother at his christening. I am told that the pictures taken on that day show a very proud family.

Throughout the reintroduction of Brian into the family the J's other boy Simon was involved and included at all times. Mrs. J. was encouraged to speak to Simon and describe what she was doing to and for Brian. Simon was later involved in helping Brian to play, and to extend his motor capacity. Simon was able to give Brian a lot of additional stimulation, playing games or merely rolling about with him on the floor.

167

Another story has a less happy outcome, but it too illustrates the special need of families with a handicapped child for extra support. In this case, the family did not receive effective help until the handicapped child was three years old. Mr. and Mrs. A. lived in a very run-down block of flats in one of the worst parts of inner London. They had initially squatted in the flat, and been subsequently offered the tenancy. Mr. and Mrs. A. had five children living with them, and only later did I become aware that there were two older children, one belonging to Mrs. A's first marriage and one belonging to both parents, but whom they had abandoned with a neighbour, some fourteen years earlier.

Mrs. A. was in her forties, an anxious woman who always appeared to be on edge. She gave the impression of having a lot of unresolved feelings that she wanted to talk about but was never able to confide.

Mr. A. was also in his forties, and had been out of work for many months. He appeared to have virtually given up any hope of working again, and spent most of his time slouched in a chair in the living room watching television.

The children at home were all boys, their ages ranging from five to fourteen years. Two boys were at secondary school and three at primary/junior. The youngest, Jack, had been born with a physical disability which was mainly a respiratory and dietary condition. His mother had had a difficult pregnancy, and said that she knew all along that something was wrong. When he was born, the parents were told that Jack's life expectancy was relatively short and that he had about a one in four chance of reaching the age of fifteen, and then a two in four chance of reaching twenty. Mr. and Mrs. A. seemed to have been offered very little practical or emotional help, and in the first two years of Jack's life he spent over 365 days in hospital. Some of these admissions were for medical reasons, but many were social admissions, because Mrs. A. felt that she was unable to cope.

When I took over the case I could see that both parents were still consumed with guilt about having brought a disabled child into the world. They were at a loss to know what to do with the child and their feelings about him, and how to cope with the jealousy of the next youngest child. Joe was only eighteen months older than Jack, and resented the attention that his younger brother was getting. He constantly claimed to be ill, and started acting in strange ways. It was easy to see that he had every cause to be angry and jealous, as his parents gave in to every demand that Jack made, whether it was for an ice-cream or for Joe's toys and books. In fact his jealousy had grown to become virtual hatred for his brother and a rivalry for his mother's affection that she simply could not handle.

With regular support however, the A's began to cope a little better, and Jack's admissions to hospital diminished. I managed to find him a place in a local day nursery, where he mixed with "normal" children but had nursing staff on hand should he need it. This inclusion in ordinary provision did a lot to alter the A's perspective of the situation: if Jack could go to a normal nursery and cope there, perhaps he did not need to be treated quite as specially as they thought? But Jack had been used to getting his own way and had worked out for himself that if he shouted loudly and long enough he got what he wanted. At the nursery this was not acceptable and a great deal of work had to be done with him to build up any kind of self-control or self-discipline.

At home, however, his mum continued to give Jack all he asked for, even though she knew that chocolate and biscuits had been strictly forbidden by the doctor. Mr. A. left most of the day to day handling of Jack to his wife. At the same time Jack became an excuse for increasing demands of the whole family. It was because of him they felt they should be re-housed; because of him they should have extra Social Security and then, because of him that the other children's toys got broken and had to be replaced.

Both parents said that their own health was suffering because of Jack, and that they could not control him although at the nursery all the reports said that he was now a well-behaved and sociable little boy.

The next shock for the family came when Jack was accepted at an ordinary local school. I think they had expected that he would need "special" provision somewhere a long way away. It seemed that the better Jack coped the worse his parents did.

The A's requested on two occasions that Jack be taken into care, and when I complied with their requests and made suitable arrangements, changed their minds at the eleventh hour. In the end their feelings of guilt could not permit them to take the final step and to "give him up" as Mr. A. put it, although they could not accept him either. It is possible that if the A's had had access to help and advice in the first two years of Jack's life, they might have been able to resolve their conflicts better, and either integrated him more fully into the family, or surrendered him to care by others.

Unfortunately, at the time of writing, it still seems to be largely a question of luck whether families like the two that I have described get the right kind of help at the right time, or not. Many Social work training courses in "disability" and the problems surrounding it are an extra option. When it is included on the curriculum, it is all too often covered in a brief, superficial and academic way which totally fails to convey any of the trauma suffered by the individual and his or her family. And many social service departments themselves give the problems of the handicapped very low priority, sometimes lumped in with those of the "elderly".

Estimates of the total number of people with a disability in the U.K. vary greatly, but a figure around two million is frequently mentioned, and even this figure is thought to be an under-estimate. The disabled therefore constitute one of the biggest minorities in the country, and one of the least regarded. The integration of people with a disability is something which is talked about, as a fashionable subject for conferences or debates, but very little real commitment has been made to this ideal by our society as a whole, and by successive Governments in particular. As a social worker I work hard to convince parents that their child, although he may be physically or mentally different from others, has as much right to education and employment as other people. Then, as if to prove me a liar, their child is sent away to a "special school"; denied vocational training; and barred from any but the dreariest jobs.

I fully accept that there is a need for some special schools, and that there are some disabilities that cannot be dealt with in ordinary schools. But I think these children should be seen as the exception rather than the rule. The Warnock Report[IX] points out that many children with a disability can be educated in their home communities within ordinary schools, and a concerted effort must now be made to allow this to happen. How will the handicapped ever become integrated members of a neighbourhood, or a family for that matter, if they are continually sent away to some specialist provision? The isolation I felt when home on school holidays I know is shared by hundreds of contemporary school children with disabilities. What is more, the standard of education obtaining in special schools remains generally lower than in ordinary schools, children already handicapped find themselves with the added disadvantage of having insufficient paper qualifications. I, for example left my school with two "O" levels and a grade one G.S.E. If I had continued my normal education and not gone blind, I might well have been expected to pass five to ten "O" levels, and "A" levels too.

There have been many changes and improvements in the special education of the visually handicapped since I was at school some thirteen years ago, but pupils wishing to attend Worcester

College for Boys (and Chorley Wood its equivalent for girls), still have to sit an entrance examination not unlike the old 11-plus. The results are still judged on a "pass" or "fail" basis and failure at that early age still has for the blind the long-term academic and career repercussions that have been rejected for non-disabled children.

When I was at school for example (and from what I know of blind education today the picture is not fundamentally altered) the jobs that we hoped for were very specific, and presented in a kind of league table: at the top were shorthand typing and audio typing, followed by telephony, piano tuning and engineering. The rest were regarded only as candidates for sheltered workshop employment. But for those who attended the "grammar" schools, the list of employment options seemed to start where ours left off. Shorthand typing was at the bottom of the ladder, the better options being physiotherapy, computer programming, teaching, social work, the law.

So while Worcester and Chorleywood pupils are expected to take their "A" levels and to go on to some form of Higher Education, in most of the schools for the V.H., pupils are still lucky if they emerge with more than one or two "O" level or C.S.E. passes. Even now, in many V.H. schools, maths are still not taught even up to G.S.E. standard.

One of the most encouraging changes I have become aware of in recent years is the growing number of V.H. children of all ages who are already being educated in ordinary schools. In one county there are some fifty children attending ordinary schools, and this in spite of the fact that a special school actually exists within its boundaries. More education authorities could seriously consider following this example.

The social attitudes in V.H. schools have begun to alter. I recently visited the Royal Edinburgh School for the Blind, for instance, and was impressed by many of the social and academic advances that have been made there. Some of the changes are small, but nevertheless they have greatly altered the conditions of life for the children. The school for example seeks to use as many outside facilities and contacts as possible instead of importing them into the school as was done in the past, and keeping the boundaries of school life narrow and inward looking. Many of the children live in small separate units, so that a distinction is drawn between school and "home". Some schools now even arrange for their older pupils to have work experience prior to leaving school in the same way as many comprehensive schools do for their fifth-year pupils.

Yet I have also seen the disturbing mannerisms in bright, educated young blind people today that so upset me when I first saw them among the pupils at Linden Lodge: mannerisms such as rocking, eye-poking or finger flicking. And I wonder how many of these mannerisms would have developed and survived if the child had been in a sighted environment, where his peers would have been the main agents of correction or ridicule? I also know that too many children are still being separated from their families, causing the breaking of emotional ties that can never be repaired and leave psychological scars which last well into adult life.

As for employment, the situation is little better. Inevitably I suppose, as the number of unemployed in the country as a whole increases, so too does the number (in somewhat higher proportions) of people with a disability who are out of work. Many companies and Government departments at the best of times fall well short of employing their quota of registered disabled workers. The argument usually put forward is that nobody with suitable qualifications or of the right standard applies. Since this is so mainly because the basic standard of education in many of the special schools is so poor, the disabled find themselves in a kind of Catch 22 situation: they do not have the right qualifications for the job, but at the same time do not have easy access to the education which provides those qualifications.

However, the employment mobility which a good basic standard of education can give the visually handicapped person is evidenced by a recent survey undertaken for the Royal National Institute for the Blind by Michael Butler.[x] Mr. Butler looked at approximately 200 students who had emerged from further education (college or university) between 1969 and 1978. The students studied were thought to represent virtually the total number of blind students, and the majority of partially sighted students, completing full-time F.E. courses during this period. A very high proportion of the students came from Worcester and Chorleywood. Over 50 percent of the students had gone into either the teaching or social work professions, and the remainder had entered one or other of the professions listed earlier in this chapter, or such others as personnel management; economics and so on. Only nine were unemployed.

The picture for the vast majority of the 10,000 or so working visually handicapped population in Britain, however, was not so encouraging. According to government figures published up to 1975, the percentage of unemployed amongst the V.H. was considerably higher than the national average. With the scheduled cuts in government spending and the shrinking overall job market for unskilled people, the employment prospects for the non-qualified blind is likely to get very much worse, especially in view of the fact that there are so many jobs for which blind people cannot qualify: driving jobs, for instance, and many of the unskilled labouring or clerical jobs for which sight is essential.

It seems more and more clear that further education opportunities hold the key to providing the V.H. person with the skills and qualifications which prospective employers or colleges may require. Perhaps some form of positive discrimination may be appropriate, whereby V.H. applicants for courses are given special consideration when it comes to the allocation of places. This does not mean that standards should be lowered to accommodate the V.H., but that the criteria for entry on to courses may be revised so as to enable as many V.H. as possible the opportunity of obtaining qualifications and examinations, or merely a basic standard of education.

Any changes such as these are no good in isolation. There have to be changes both in attitudes and in opportunities if education itself is to open some of the doors which I, and many other people with a disability, would like to see opened. True integration is a long way off, and if it is to become a reality will depend just as much on the efforts of the disabled themselves as on the able-bodied.

Challenges and frustrations arise virtually every day, and the will to meet and overcome them is neither easily acquired nor, if there is the will, there is no guarantee that a way can be found! The biggest barriers in life are often ones we place there for ourselves! In the case of people with disabilities however, there are many more barriers and obstacles placed in the way by other people.

What of the future?

I do not know what the future holds in store for me. I just hope that by adopting my motto of "Where There's a Will" that the challenges to come are exciting, challenging and that I am able to realise my potential, whether it be in the sporting arena, at work or in my family life.

If you've enjoyed reading *Where There's A Will*, you might want to take a look at Mike's second book:

Don't ask me, ask the dog!:
The autobiography of Mike Brace CBE DL: Part 2

REFERENCES

[i] *Sport and Physical Recreation For The Disabled*, Disabled Living Foundation, 1970

[ii] *The Value Of Sport For The Severely Physically Handicapped*, Hexagon magazine, published by Roche Drug Co., Nov 1974

[iii] *Sports For The Disabled*, by Ken Roberts, 1974

[iv] *Shin Kicking Champion*, by Norman Croucher, Barrie & Jenkins, 1971

[v] Quoted in Ken Roberts, *Sports For The Disabled*

[vi] Op. Cit.

[vii] *Physical Disability: A Psychological Approach*, by Beatrice Wright, Harper and Row, 1960

[viii] *Stigma: Notes On The Management Of Spoiled Identity*, by Erving Goffman, Aronson, 1974

[ix] *Report Of The Committee Of Enquiry Into The Education Of Handicapped Children and Young People*, 1979

[x] *Visually Handicapped Students*, by Michael Butler, RNIB, 1979

46959714R00106

Printed in Poland
by Amazon Fulfillment
Poland Sp. z o.o., Wrocław